39102000084722
4/24/2008
McCarthy, Todd.
Fast women :

D0482055

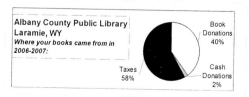

Albany County Public Library
Laramie, WY
*Where your books came from in
2006-2007:*

Book
Donations
40%

Taxes
58%

Cash
Donations
2%

FAST
WOMEN

THE LEGENDARY LADIES
OF RACING

FAST WOMEN

THE LEGENDARY LADIES
OF RACING

TODD McCARTHY

miramax books

HYPERION

NEW YORK

Albany County
Public Library
Laramie, Wyoming

Copyright © 2007 Todd McCarthy

All rights reserved. No part of this book may be used or reproduced in
any manner whatsoever without the written permission of the
Publisher.
Printed in the United States of America. For information address
Hyperion, 77 West 66th Street, New York, NY 10023-6298

ISBN 1-4013-5202-2

First Edition
10 9 8 7 6 5 4 3 2 1

To my mother and father,

Barbara and Dan McCarthy

FAST
WOMEN
THE LEGENDARY LADIES
OF RACING

LADIES, START YOUR ENGINES

Sports cars often create their own trips. You don't have them because you have to go somewhere, you have them to give you a reason to go somewhere.

—DENISE McCLUGGAGE

I have to have this," the determined young woman said to the friend who had taken her up to Van Ness Avenue in San Francisco on a fateful day in 1949. "I have to have this." It was, indisputably, love at first sight, provoking a need for instant gratification such as she hadn't felt since she was a little girl. Denise McCluggage, a newcomer at the *Chronicle*, was standing with her colleague Barney Clark on the showroom floor of Kjell Qvale's newly opened British Motor Cars. The object of her desire was a brand-new MG TC—black, right-hand drive, with long running boards in the manner of pre-war cars, tonno cover and hinged windscreen that could be laid flat—that had arrived in one of the first shipments of new English cars since the war ended. She had seen the MG—the very same one, she later figured out—in a *Life* magazine article about the sporty foreign cars that were beginning to hit American roads, and was struck by a full-page photograph of a woman driving the car *under* a lumber carrier, something quite unthinkable in the boat-size sedans issuing from Detroit at the time.

No doubt about it, $2400 was out of reach for the pugnacious, pixieish tomboy—two years out of Mills College—who had cajoled and charmed and pitched (as in baseball) her way onto a paper with no interest in women staffers. But the next day, when she returned to gaze upon the car again, Denise discovered that the English pound had been severely devalued overnight, bringing the price down to $1850. That was that. Daddy in Kansas got an unexpected phone call, was persuaded to give his daughter a loan, and within the week Denise was speeding down Route 1 with a New York theater lad desperate to rendezvous with Tennessee Williams while the playwright was in Los Angeles. With the top down and the windscreen clamped upon the bonnet, they donned goggles and jackets and were off, through Santa Cruz and Monterey and on to Big Sur, where Denise thrilled to the sight of the coast dropping off precipitously just beneath her right elbow while her chum scrunched down miserably as traffic assaulted him near the center line. She made the return trip on her own the next day, not realizing at the time that in Los Angeles she was leaving behind the nascent hotbed of American sports car racing culture. But this first impulsive journey was her initial lesson in how sports cars alter your life and influence the roads taken.

Across the continent, it was the same, only different, for a striking, six-foot blond doyenne of Pennsylvania society who found herself at the center of a revolution among the horsy set: Evelyn Mull and her husband John were throwing over the fox hunt and steeplechase for noisy foreign automobiles. Shock and dismay overcame the blue bloods in 1949 when new European cars began joining the horses in the Mulls' stables at their resplendent family estate of Moshannon Farm at Malvern, just west of Philadelphia. The first interloper was a French Simca Aronde, then an automatic Citroen to replace a De Soto station wagon and, most decisively, a gorgeous XK120, the first of what were to be sixteen Jaguars John and Evelyn would acquire over the years, usually the result of a personal visit to the factory at Browns Lane, Coventry. Their riding-and-jumping daughter Nonny came undone when their horse trailer was transformed into a van for transporting sports cars to races.

That first Jaguar was so gloriously powerful that it

didn't take John, a temperamental, intellectual industrialist in his early fifties—a dozen years older than his wife—long to decide it was made for something more than just cruising the rural back roads near home. Organized racing on public roads was then struggling to make a comeback at a handful of venues in the East, including Thompson Speedway in the far northeastern corner of Connecticut. A demanding but not treacherous two-mile asphalt course through pleasantly hilly terrain, it was a perfect place to test one's skills, and when John announced his intentions of entering the novice race on Memorial Day 1953, Evelyn agreed to go along, a scheme up her sleeve.

She calculated her dialogue and the timing of it impeccably. When they arrived at their rural Connecticut motel after the journey up from Pennsylvania in the XK120, Evelyn told John she would be driving in the parallel women's novice race. "You can't," her husband said dismissively. "You've never raced before." "You've never done it before either," she countered. "If you can do it, so can I." "All right," John replied, "maybe it will teach you a lesson. Go ahead."

After obliging race officials by installing seat belts in the Jag, the Mulls quickly began learning the difference between simply driving fast and running side by side against other drivers just as determined as you to win. First up on Saturday afternoon was the ladies' race. Evelyn saw at once that she had the biggest car in the field and was given a handicap to more fairly match her against the MGs and Porsches. With one exception, the other women were competition first-timers like her. Once off the starting line, she felt confident and strong and had little trouble outgunning the smaller cars around her, although her lack of expertise became painfully evident when she failed to downshift through the turns, smoking the car's already mediocre brakes in the process. With every lap, she became more exhilarated; far from fearing the other cars around her, she loved taking them on, maneuvering past them and watching them disappear in her rearview mirror. She completed the ten laps in second place, trailing only the MG driven by the one woman with some racing experience, Carlye Ann "Scotty" Scott. For Evelyn, the experience was life altering. She told her husband, who finished in the middle of the pack in the male novice race, that nothing was going to hold her back now. To be sure, she had a lot to learn. But that summer, which the Mulls spent traversing the eastern seaboard to compete in three more races and two hill climbs, the entire structure of their lives changed; henceforth, like real race car drivers, they "would live from race to race."

In yet another part of the country, a car-crazy young woman made her racing debut in a very different setting—

on a frozen lake. Ruth Levy had always loved speed and the way the exertion it required defeated the cold of Minnesota winters. She enjoyed ice boating with her brother, was the only girl in the neighborhood with racing skates, and as a teenager had been drawn to the wealthy but vaguely disreputable boys who hung out at garages and raced hot rods down alleys. Ruth spent much of her young life trying to reconcile her deep love for her family with her irresistible urge to rebel and go her own way. At twenty-four she was divorced with two daughters, owned an MG TC and joined a local sports car club. But it had never occurred to her to race until a friend dared her to prove her worth in the annual Midwestern curiosity known as the St. Paul Winter Carnival Ice Race.

The course was snowplowed into a shape that, from the air, resembled a massive letter *B* upon the frozen surface of Lake Phalen, a long, peanut-shaped recreation spot just east of the city center. Borrowing a faster MG TC, Ruth drew plenty of attention before the race and even more after she won the ladies event. Fearless from the beginning, Ruth slipped and slid her way around the curvy course, stayed out of snowbanks and hay bales and kicked slush and ice in the faces of anyone who got close behind her. "I was brought up driving on ice as a kid, so there wasn't much to it," she says. "It was kind of like dirt racing. You'd just put it into big slides on the turns." Thrilled and impressed with herself, Ruth became the town's driving celebrity. As with Denise and Evelyn, the arrival of cars in her life became its primary determining factor, and after the ice thawed she and some of the boys hit the season's regional Midwestern races, where she did well. It took about a year to figure out how to reconcile being a single mother of two with pursuing her new dream of racing where racing mattered, but once she did, she was on her way with the top down to Los Angeles, where she arrived like a gunslinger from a far-off town, sized everybody up and put them in their place.

It's not unusual for young people to be drawn to cars, particularly exotic, sexy ones that go fast and attract other people to you. If there's a sense of rebellion attached to it, a means of asserting some individuality, setting yourself apart and going your own way, so much the better. Still, in the early 1950s, a time of settling and retrenchment, women racing cars didn't seem like a terribly likely development.

But in one of the wonderful paradoxes in a decade rife with them, it was precisely during that time, most of all between roughly 1953 and 1958, that women raced in numbers and with an excellence unheard of until then and arguably unmatched to this day. It was a privileged moment in the grand sweep of American automobile racing, a small window of time when the sport was accessible to virtually anyone with a desire to pursue it; if you had a car and were good enough, you could drive it to a track and race. Women included.

This had emphatically not been the case up to then. Throughout the twentieth century the racing establishment in its various incarnations across the globe had thrown up innumerable barriers to prevent a woman from obliging any man—or men, collectively—to suffer the indignity of coming in second to her behind the wheel of a car. Most commonly, the barrier took the form of an outright ban on women competing in officially sanctioned car races; this was true in the United States from 1909, and in other prominent racing nations for long periods. Many reasons or, to state it more accurately, excuses were advanced: Women weren't strong enough to handle the heavy, unwieldy early race cars (sometimes true); women weren't mechanically inclined (not always the case, although neither were some male drivers), and female injuries and fatalities were bad publicity for the sport overall and were imagined to discourage car sales to women (everyone knew it was a risky undertaking). The most memorable objection to women taking up motorcar racing was that made by the grandees of the English sporting world in the early years—that since women were not permitted as race horse jockeys, there was no reason to alter the rules simply because the means of conveyance now had an engine (reasoning of incontestable consistency if nothing else). It would not have mattered to the dukes and lords who arbitrated such things that there were any number of record-setting female aviators and even speedboat drivers.

All the same, some pockets of opportunity were seized upon by women in the British Isles and on the Continent during the 1920s and 1930s. Between the wars, auto racing in Europe remained largely the domain of a wealthy elite, and in rarified circles general rules and standards could be bent for the privileged. Where cars were concerned, class and money sometimes conferred certain privileges, as borne out by the thrilling careers of the exceptional women who raced at the Brooklands track in England during the 1930s. In the United States, by contrast, auto racing took the low road of treacherous dirt and board tracks and barnstorming county-fair contests; except for the Indy, the sport resembled a rude cousin of circuses and amusement parks, with mechanics as drivers and rubes for fans. The split can be seen even now, between the refined sophistication of Formula 1, the dominant international category since the 1950s, and the common-man orientation of American

NASCAR, an organization with moonshine driver roots, which still covertly operates on the principle of inducing legions of Jethros and Billy Bobs to imagine they drive cars pretty much like the ones they see on the track, even as they know they can't drive their cars at two hundred miles per hour.

But given the strict rules and regulations that pertained in the entrenched categories of automotive competition after World War II—F1, Indy, NASCAR/stock car, dragstrip, endurance tests such as the 24 Hours of Le Mans and the Mille Miglia—it took a new branch of racing for the sport to assume momentarily what was arguably its purest form, the one that was almost certainly the most wide open and fun from a participants' point of view. "Sporty car" racing in the United States was looked down upon at first by "real" race drivers as an amateur pastime, which indeed it was, in its infancy in the late 1940s and early 1950s, and a status that some of its adherents fought bitterly for it to remain forever after. Its casual character was inescapably a major part of its charm; at the outset its organization was as ad hoc as its venues, which ranged from hastily laid out road courses through pristine countryside to rough, hay bale lined Air Force bases. For years, most racers drove themselves to the tracks in the very cars in which they would compete.

Naturally, it didn't hurt to have money, and since

most of the East Coast buyers of the first hot European cars imported after World War II were wealthy, sports car racing started out as an elite endeavor, joining the list of such upscale pursuits as equestrian competition and yachting. All the same, the cost was not restrictive. In 1950, $2500 or less bought a gorgeous new MG TC, the entry-level car of choice for the majority of aspiring racers, from Phil Hill to Carroll Shelby, and almost every woman with a taste for elegant speed. If competitive racing was something you really wanted to do and you reordered your priorities accordingly, it was not financially out of bounds, a fact borne out by the preponderance of middle-class working people who swelled the ranks of racers on the West Coast through the 1950s.

Nor were there exclusionary rules, and it was this irreducibly egalitarian situation that permitted American women to get involved in automobile racing for the first time in significant numbers. Some prejudices, assumptions, and expectations needed to be overcome: men accustomed to "track fluff" being the only women around racing had to readjust their thinking; male drivers worried how inexperienced women would react in tight situations at high speeds; and masculine egos were inevitably threatened by the possibility of a woman showing them up.

But by and large, the streaming of women into the sports racing scene took place with remarkable ease and an admirable matter-of-factness, especially when compared with the male intransigence on one side and the feminist confrontationalism on the other that was to mark some aspects of the increased female sports profile in subsequent decades. At first, sensibly, women were largely confined to "ladies' races," because an experience-generating training ground in competition was needed to weed out the unqualified and provide valuable track time to relative beginners. Eventually, however, more races opened up in which men and women could run against one another, the ideal sought by the most capable and ambitious of drivers. In how many other sports has this ever happened? None, obviously, in which brute strength, size, and speed are decisive factors, which covers most athletic endeavors, and scarcely any other either, including golf, bowling, table tennis—even billiards and pool.

This begs the often-debated question of whether or not auto racing qualifies as a real sport, one requiring conditioning and preparation on a par with athletic endeavors that don't involve sitting for hours on end. Denise McCluggage argued the matter repeatedly with the all-star sports reporter staff at the *New York Herald Tribune,* including with her disapproving colleague Red Smith. The issue remains such a contentious one that, fifty years later, Denise backs up her opinion by revealing how veteran sports broadcaster Chris Economaki personally verified with Ernest Hemingway a comment the writer had allegedly once made but never wrote down, that being, "There are only three real sports—boxing, bullfighting and automobile racing. The rest are merely games."

Hemingway regrettably never wrote about auto racing, but then he only wrote about things he knew well and he never drove fast cars or hung around tracks. In *Death in the Afternoon*, he postulated that bullfighting is the most tragic of sports. If this is so, then auto racing must be the most existential; the solitary participant expends furious energy to remain constantly on the brink between triumph and disaster for arbitrary periods of time that can be as long as twenty-four hours and in a state composed of equal parts prodigious concentration and draining monotony, where the slightest error or errant rock or patch of oil can be instantly fatal, and with the goal simply to wind up where you started after going around and around and around. To what end, the coolly detached observer may ask, and to what point?

Most men race cars to win, many simply because it is the fastest and most exciting way to do what men have always done, first on foot, then on horseback and in chariots, as well as on every other animal and vehicle that proved feasible to provide a ride. Stirling Moss, surely one of the top five race car drivers of all time and among the most analytical, told Ken Purdy forty years ago that he doubted a woman could become a genuinely great racing driver, but not for lack of strength, ability or courage. "It's just that women are almost never *personally* competitive. In rallying, which is a less demanding form of racing, there are women who are very good indeed, there are women who will beat all but the top men, and beat them easily. But rallying is running against the clock, and women do that sort of thing very well." Josie von Neumann, the fastest woman in American racing in the early 1950s and the first to drive Ferraris, agreed. "I do not think the best of the women drivers can ever be as good as the best of the men," she said in 1959, by which time she had become the first woman authorized by the United States Auto Club to compete in a nationally sanctioned race. "They will always be more cautious because of their terrific drive for self-preservation. But some of us can be very good."

Many may feel that attitudes have changed, and there is little doubt that some women athletes in sports, ranging from tennis and skiing to volleyball and softball, display a killer approach that matches that of the men. But Moss—whose mother was an ace rally and trials driver, having won the 1936 Ladies Experts Trial, and younger sister Pat was European Rally Champion in 1958—felt that in general, up to that point, "[W]omen will not compete, as the Spanish say, mano a mano, hand to hand. They will not go into really brutal competition with another person, they will not, or they cannot, as a rule, reach the highest plane of the competitive urge, where a man will say: 'Right, now I've had enough of hanging about, now I'll have a go, now we're going to separate the men from the boys here.' No, they won't do that. Mind, I'm not saying that's wrong, or a bad thing. I'm just saying that's the way it is. When someone says that if women ran the governments of the world there'd be no wars, no argument comes from *my* corner of the room. It's probably true."

Because there were essentially no American women race car drivers in the 1930s and 1940s, those who came along afterward had no role models and couldn't, and didn't, grow up dreaming about racing; it was not something they were expected to do, nor was it anything anyone else wanted them to do—their mothers, their husbands, the male drivers. There was no encouragement, no one doting over them saying, "Come on, darling, you can do it, I know you can do it." It all came from within. It was a desire, a need—"I *must* have that car, I *must* race"—that was self-generated and self-propelled. It became, at a certain moment, what they wanted to do and what they had to do. It was action, speed, kicks, life lived more intensely for a few minutes or hours, just as it was for the most famous drivers on the planet.

When they took it up, there was no formal training to be had; they just had to start doing it and discover if they were any good. The average ones stayed in it—if they did—for the same reasons most sports car drivers did so: for the fun, the social boost, the weekend excitement. But for the ones who proved they could win races or reliably finish in the top three, the sport became something more and they wanted to win. A few of them won regularly, and three or four beat serious male competition once in a while. Licensing of female racers rose dramatically through the mid to late 1950s; for a moment, it seemed that the future was arriving.

And then, suddenly and without their having seen it coming, it was over, sooner than seemed possible. The window, which had opened so wide that all the fast young women had to do was climb right through it, closed again; not only did the women find a glass ceiling preventing their continuing up through the ranks, but there was glass all around through which they could see their male friends and competitors continue doing what they all used to do together. The story was different for each driver, but the effect on all of them was the same: The pressures of money, sponsorship, and the sport's shift to professionalism pushed them aside, and there was nowhere else for them to go.

◻ ◻ ◻

It was a single photograph that seduced me. The picture on the wall of a friend's family home was simply of an open-cockpit sports car of 1950s vintage whizzing along in front of bystanders blurred by speed, an ordinary shot but captivating enough to inspire a closer look. Something about the erect, slim posture of the driver was a bit unusual. There was a fine-cut elegance to the nose, mouth and chin, barely discernable at a distance but sufficiently pronounced to suggest distinction. White shirt cuffs emerged at just the right length from the arms of what looked like a sport coat, and the hands on the steering wheel, positioned at the correct ten and two o'clock, were sheathed in leather driving gloves. Sunglasses, not goggles, were in place beneath a helmet resembling a dark polo cap, beneath which . . . hold on, isn't that a hair-bun tucked up under the back of the helmet? Could that be a woman racing the car? Suddenly, the photograph became far more intriguing, and deeply mysterious.

Two questions leaped to mind simultaneously: Who is that, and what is she doing? Even in this long shot and encumbered by clothes and gear, it was clear that the

17

woman was exceptional, doubtless a beauty; the posture
and profile held a poise and regal bearing that suggested
Grace Kelly. It was no wonder, then, that the woman in
question, Evelyn Mull, was another blue-blooded WASP
who lived on an estate just a few miles from the Philadelphia home of Kelly's parents.

All the more pressing, therefore, became the second
question. Evelyn's daughter Ellie, at whose ranch near
Santa Fe I encountered the photograph, and granddaughter Cary soon filled me in about Evelyn, who had
died some years earlier. She had become one of the leading women sports car drivers of the 1950s—the best of
1957, by the Sports Car Club of America's ranking system. She also wrote the first book about American
women in racing, an extended pamphlet, really, light-
hearted but informative. In 1958, when it was published,
there were sixty-one women licensed to race by the
Sports Car Club of America, an equal number who raced
unofficially, and perhaps hundreds more who devoted
themselves to rallies; Evelyn confidently expected the
number to double or triple within another year or two.
So even she couldn't see the endgame that was already
in motion.

I was introduced to this unknown world by a be-
guiling photograph, one that comes close to summing up
the essential quality of the sport—grace, purpose, and ex-

hilaration in action. A couple of days later, I went down the road to Santa Fe to meet the most accomplished and knowledgeable woman of her generation in the automotive world, Denise McCluggage. Still in the thick of the automotive scene—at age seventy-nine, in late 2006, she drove the final leg of the Mercedes Bluetec Paris–Beijing run—she is a fine photographer and writer, passionate and acutely informed on the arts, politics, and many other subjects. Whether she would admit it or not, Denise has lived one of the most enviable of modern lives—she has seen the world, known exceptional people during the most interesting of times, and forged career trails where none had gone before her. She would no doubt scoff at this notion; none of her recollections of past exploits and legendary friends betray a prejudiced insistence that things were better then.

And yet it's so evident that they were. Even a dry, factual account of locations, car models, and participants' names evokes a romantic resonance that little since can match: Pebble Beach, Bridgehampton, Bahamas Speed Week, Jaguar XK120, Porsche Spyder 550, Allard-Cadillac, Juan Manuel Fangio, Stirling Moss, Phil Hill. Is it possible to consider those days without permitting even the slightest hint of nostalgia to creep in? Some sociologists and historians might stress the well-known biases, the racial and sexual restrictions of the period, the political paranoia and social conformism. These things existed and impacted all lives to one degree or another.

But the women who raced in the 1950s reflect a neglected flip side to the story. What happened on a macro, societal scale in the 1960s had started on a micro, personal level more than a decade earlier. What may have appeared at first glance to be composed of upper-class, elitist ingredients—fancy sports cars, snooty addresses, an aristocracy of speed—increasingly came to assume the character of a very particular form of bohemia, a rarified strain, perhaps, but one marked by a pronounced iconoclasm and a fair-minded, inclusive spirit within the frame of an excitingly fluid meritocracy. As the film director Howard Hawks, the subject of my last book, might have said, you were welcome in the club *if you were good enough*. No question that East Coast sports car racing was largely for the rich, but even there, the Mulls and others ran against the grain of their culture by throwing over traditional aristocratic recreational pursuits for a noisy, dirty, populist sport commonly identified with grease monkeys. And the openness of the scene was such that outsiders and interlopers like Denise McCluggage, from the truly bohemian worlds of San Francisco and then Greenwich Village, could show up and infiltrate the group; she forever remained both an outsider and the ultimate insider. Desire and enthusiasm were the first qualifications, and then skill.

Because there was no preexisting sports car racing infrastructure, the situation was far more open and democratic on the West Coast. It all started as club racing, in an environment where "club" held no restrictive or class-based country-club connotations; aircraft companies had their racing clubs, as did MG owners, particular town residents, and so on. These groups were comprised largely of working people who drove whenever they could, mostly on weekends, with the Women's Sports Car Club, formed in 1953, becoming involved initially on the administrative, organizational, and social end of things. When there was enough demand, and in spite of some manly grunting and harrumphing, ladies' events became part of race days, and that was that.

The world of sports car racing in the 1950s possessed a beautiful and paradoxical character. It was an elegant pursuit open to anyone who cared to engage it and on whatever basis you wanted; you could visit on weekends or succumb to it entirely; you could change spark plugs for a living in a shop Monday through Friday and race against Phil Hill, Carroll Shelby or, one year, James Dean on Saturday and Sunday; you could do it just for the fun and thrills or take it very seriously indeed, with an eye on international competition. Just as happened for Evelyn and John, for Denise and for Ruth, whimsical yet necessary purchases of cars they fancied provided quite a few others with passports into a land that, in the early 1950s, hadn't fully taken shape yet, the likes of which had never existed before and which, by the end of the decade, would mutate into something else entirely.

Attempting to strip away every shred of nostalgia and toss out every pair of rose-colored glasses, it remains impossible not to conclude that the 1950s represented a golden time for racing, and for women's participation in it. Pushed to the mat with her arm twisted behind her, Denise is finally forced to admit it: "It was a unique time. The beginnings of things usually are. People are always saying, 'Your time was really the best.' And it was."

FIRST RACES:
FROM CHAUFFEUSSES
TO SPEEDERETTES

Good driving has nothing to do with sex. It's all above the collar.

—ANNE RAMSEY

The first automobile races worthy of the name took place in France and the United States in 1895. In France, the leader in all things automotive during the sport's infancy, Emile Levassor stayed awake for the two days and forty-eight minutes, June 11–13, it took him to drive the 732 miles from Paris to Bordeaux and back in his two-cylinder, four-horsepower Panhard-Levassor, only to be told at the finish line that he was disqualified on the technicality that his vehicle had just two seats rather than the requisite four; it remains unrecorded why he was told this at the end rather than at the beginning of the race, or what he said in response. The first such contest in the United States unintentionally became a two-part affair. The event, originally scheduled for November 2, was redubbed an exhibition run when only two contestants proved ready. In the end, only one finished, as Oscar Mueller, in his father's Mueller-Benz, made the ninety-two-mile trip from Chicago's South Side north to Waukegan and back in eight hours, forty-four minutes. The actual race was run, if *race* is the word, on Thanksgiving Day, November 28, 1895, a fifty-four-mile round-trip from Chicago to Evanston, the first suburb to the north. Having run aground in the exhibition, this time driver Frank Duryea, in a car he made with his brother Charles, was not to be denied, averaging less than seven miles per hour over the ten hours, twenty-three minutes total, or seven hours and fifty-three minutes of actual driving it took to fight his way through more than a half foot of snow and slush along the shores of Lake Michigan. Although crowds had lined the roadway throughout the day, only a few dozen braved the cold of the evening to await the winner, who received a $2000 prize for his efforts.

These events were far from scintillating, but they were a start nonetheless to a sport that would become one of the most popular of the coming century. Auto racing developed more quickly in Europe, where competition among vehicles went way back; until the nineteenth century, nothing on wheels went nearly as fast as chariots, the speed passion of the ancients. In the fourteenth century, some Italians began trying to marry windmill-like devices to gears and wheels to develop propulsion, without pronounced success. By 1769–70, nearly a century's worth of trial and error with the steam engine had resulted in the first invention able to move under its own power, an eight-thousand-pound monstrosity devised to drag cannons around Paris at two miles per hour. Only slightly less unwieldy were some steam-driven American iron giants created before the Civil War. In 1878, a 231-mile "race" sponsored by the State of Wisconsin, with a $10,000 prize attached, was able to draw seven registrants and two "steam wagons" that actually turned up to compete. In the end, only one of them managed to last the distance, making it from Green Bay to its home in Oshkosh in thirty-three hours and twenty-seven minutes.

But the insurmountable limitation of any steam-powered means of locomotion was its weight and consequent need to travel on something flatter and far sturdier than cobblestones or dirt. So iron tracks were laid and on them steam-driven trains remained, while countless inventors in many countries vainly labored for a hundred years to make their names and fortunes by finding the key to the internal combustion engine. They tried gunpowder. They tried coal. Etienne Lenoir manufactured a gasoline-powered car and drove it from Paris to Joinville in 1862, but it was too cumbersome and had the power of only half a horse and that's as far as it ever went. Separately, in 1885, Gottlieb Daimler and Karl Benz made workable petroleum-powered vehicles in Germany, Daimler a wooden motorcycle and Benz a three-wheeler; in 1888, Karl's wife, Berta, became the first woman known to drive a gas-propelled vehicle when she coaxed the trike sixty-two miles from Mannheim to Pforzheim to visit her mother. The first gas-driven wheels in the United States consisted of a horse buggy fitted with a one-cylinder engine by the Massachusetts-based Charles and Frank Duryea, the latter the very same who won the Chicago race two years later. Thirteen Duryea cars were manufactured in 1896, all of which were sold and five of which competed in the first closed-circuit auto race held in the United States, at Narragansett Park, Rhode Island, that September before a reported crowd of fifty thousand.

At this stage, though, European car design and mechanics, not to mention racing, were far ahead of their counterparts in America. Auto races along public thoroughfares between European cities followed in the path of bicycling events that had held the public in thrall for the previous decade. In the beginning, it was a feat in itself to build and operate a motorized vehicle strong and reliable enough to run any distance without breaking down; the first sanctioned automobile event in France was not a race per se but a "reliability run" between Paris and Rouen in 1894, sponsored by the newspaper *Le Petit Journal* to demonstrate that the newfangled invention could be "safe, easily controllable and reasonably economical to run." In Europe as in the United States, manufacturers themselves took part in events; Gottlieb Daimler drove in an 1896 London–Brighton run, and Charles Rolls in England, Ettore Bugatti in Italy, and Levassor and the Renault brothers in France drove competitively as a way of testing and upgrading their machinery. The drivers, amateurs all by virtue of the field's newness, were almost by necessity wealthy, as others could scarcely afford to indulge in something as frivolous and impractical as a horseless carriage. Some aristocrats, including the Baron Henri de Rothschild, entered competitions under pseudonyms to mask their identities.

In the first years of a new endeavor almost freakish for its unreliable conveyances, shattering noise, and potential for violence, it's not surprising that only sketchy, sporadic records were kept, the names of many participants unknown. By common consensus, the first female race car driver was a certain Madame Laumaille, who finished twenty-seventh in an 1898 Marseille–Nice contest. The following year, a Mademoiselle Labrousse, whose Christian name similarly went unregistered, came in fifth in a dash from Paris to Spa, Belgium. In Italy, the Countess

Elsa Albrizzi took part in a Padua–Vincenza–Thiene–Bassan–Treviso–Padua race, placing ninth in a Benz.

But the first female competition driver to make a mark, to prove herself in direct competition with top male drivers, was another française, Camille du Gast. A green-eyed, light-haired, voluptuous, evidently captivating woman, Camille, who always used her maiden name in her sporting life, was one of the fabulous characters of her age, a wealthy woman who delighted in flaunting convention and was sufficiently plucky (by far the single favorite adjective used to describe female drivers at the time) to stride confidently into one male-dominated domain after another, and to succeed once she got there. Married at twenty-two and already a first-rate pianist and horsewoman, she became intrigued by more exotic pursuits when her husband, Jules Crespin, began using large gas balloons to publicize his popular stores, Dufayel; Camille gained her initial public notoriety in 1895 when she became the first woman to jump from a balloon using a parachute, a perilous endeavor then, to say the least.

Forever indulged by her husband as she pursued mountain climbing, tobogganing, fencing, and shooting, Camille learned to drive in 1900, at age thirty, and the following June entered the epochal Paris–Berlin race, a three-day, 687-mile run noted for the terrible road dust the cars kicked up. She made a huge impression when, accompanied by a diminutive dandy of a mechanic with the Proustian name of Prince du Sagan, she finished 33rd against 122 male competitors—only 47 drivers completed the trip—despite the fact that her twenty-horsepower Panhard-Levassor was only half as strong as the other vehicles. Two years later she was again the only woman among the 175 to 200 drivers who signed on for a daunting and ultimately horrific 872-mile Paris–Madrid marathon. To be run on dirt roads through towns and rural villages at a furious pace, most precariously so on the downhill straightaways, the race was broken down into four categories by vehicle weight, and drivers in all classes were required to sit on identical wooden boards. An estimated fifty thousand people converged on Versailles for the event's scheduled start at 3:30 A.M. on Sunday, May 24, 1903, and countless others crowded along rural roads and in village squares for the thrilling arrival of the dashing pacesetters of the new century.

Accoutered in goggles, leather duster, and heavy protective gear, Camille du Gast was physically indistinguishable from her male counterparts, except for one thing: Her corset required her to sit up very straight, whereas the men tended to hunker down over the wheel or, as in the case of her inescapable slight mechanic, to slump in their seats to avoid the oncoming rush of air. For the occasion, she had persuaded her husband to buy her a new thirty-horsepower De Dietrich, an advanced French make of the time but still modest compared to the ninety-horsepower Mercedes that were entered. Also driving De Dietrichs, albeit versions specially outfitted with extra-strong suspensions, were three leading British drivers, one of whom, Charles Jarrott, penned a memoir that offers the best account of the beautiful, dreadful day.

Jarrott observed that, just as some of the cars were first-rate while others were "un-safe, unsuitable and impossible," a number of the drivers knew what they were doing but too many others were rank amateurs with no qualifications. No one dared accuse Camille of this, although the leading specialized magazine of the time, *L'Auto*, sniffed: "We must confess to a feeling of doubt as to whether distance racing is quite the thing for ladies." Having the distinction of the equivalent of pole position, Jarrott was the first to start his engine and, accompanied by his mechanic, Bianchi, to make his way in the dark through the teeming mob, which grudgingly parted as he gingerly gathered speed. His dominant memory of the event was this: "Long avenues of trees, top-heavy with foliage and gaunt in their very nakedness of trunk . . . fleeting glimpses of towns and dense masses of people—mad people, insane and reckless, holding themselves in front of the bullet to be ploughed and cut and maimed to extinction, evading the inevitable at the last moment in frantic haste; overpowering relief, as each mass was passed and each chance of catastrophe escaped, and beyond all, the horrible feeling of being hunted."

After threading through ever-billowing dust and the crowds that pressed in at Chartres and elsewhere along the road, the first to arrive in Tours—which was even more jammed with picnickers, bicyclists, and flag-waving celebrants—was Louis Renault, whose brothers and partners in the pioneering French manufacturing company, Marcel and Fernand, were also in the race. A huge German named Werner in a huge Mercedes was next, followed by three De Dietrichs, one driven by Jarrott, another by Phil Stead and then the one piloted by Camille du Gast; even though she had started twenty-ninth in the field, at the near halfway point of the first day she was fifth overall.

Pressing on through more difficult terrain, and bothered everywhere by spectators who thought nothing of standing in the middle of the road, animals running about, and dust clouds making it all a haze, Renault maintained his lead and arrived in Bordeaux first, followed fifteen minutes later by Jarrott, relieved as a fox who had survived a day being pursued by dozens of dogs. There they waited for subsequent drivers, who were oddly slow in arriving. As some began turning up, rumors circulated of dreadful crashes, unimaginable carnage, and many deaths. In fact six drivers died, among them the most senior of the De Dietrich pilots, Lorraine Barrow, who rammed into a tree after abruptly turning to avoid a dog. Most shocking from the French point of view, Marcel Renault was killed, near Angouleme. As for Camille du Gast, she was still among the front-runners when, outside Libourne, she saw one of the De Dietrichs lying in a ditch; pinned under it was Stead, alive but badly hurt, who urged Camille to continue on. She wouldn't hear of it, remaining to gather people to lift the car, make him comfortable, pull away the body of Stead's dead mechanic and wait until medics arrived. After completing the remaining thirty kilometers—she earned forty-fifth place, as if it now mattered—she arrived in Bordeaux to find the remainder of the race already canceled, the cars being impounded and, in a particular irony, set to be dragged by horses to trains that would return them to Paris.

In addition to the drivers, numerous spectators—the unlucky ones among the many who so heedlessly ventured into the roads to closely observe the speed demons—had been killed, many more injured (authorities never put a final number on the casualties) and innumerable cars were destroyed. Jarrott, who credited Camille du

Gast with saving Phil Stead's life, went back over the road afterward and marveled, "not that several had been killed but that so many had escaped. Cars in fragments, cars in fields, some upside down, others with no wheels." In 1903, then, as Jarrott viewed it, "Road racing was dead. Never again would it be possible to suggest a speed event over the open roads, and the sport—which, while it was sport, was in my opinion the best of all sports—was finished. The peculiar thing about it all was that the outside world had not appreciated up to that moment that there was an element of danger in motor racing. One or two drivers had certainly been injured, but accidents were very rare; and then, suddenly, by one of those compensations which occur with all things in life, the toll was paid in one event, and so heavy was it that with a shudder and a gasp the world at large realized that motor racing might be really deadly."

The French government responded dramatically, banning open-road racing from town to town. Another, less publicized, ban was the one on Camille du Gast. She attempted to enter the French elimination races for the 1904 Gordon Bennett Cup, an annual competition founded in 1900 and sponsored by James Gordon Bennett, the flamboyant American sportsman who owned the *New York Herald* and started the Paris-based *International Herald Tribune.* In response to the Paris–Madrid fiasco, the French Commission Sportive decided to bar women entirely from racing, deciding it couldn't risk the negative publicity of a woman being badly injured or killed in an automotive event. Camille's spirited letter of protest in *L'Auto* was to no avail.

So she turned her attention to speedboats, racing the *Turquoise* out of Monaco. In 1905, in a new craft called *Camille*, she took part in the most ambitious boating event of the year, a trans-Mediterranean contest from Algiers to Toulon that no one finished; in the final section, out of Port Mahon, Minorca, a violent storm capsized or sank six of the seven boats; miraculously, all hands were rescued. Camille du Gast was declared the winner, as her boat sank closest to the French coast.

If the French outflanked the rest of the newly motorized world in its degree of automaniacal zeal, the United States rated a close second. Initially, as in France, city-to-city contests became prevalent, and rudimentary races became attractions at fairs and carnival sites. But it took a wealthy young man who could legitimately lay claim to having been America's first automotive speed freak to set up the first significant international event comparable to those that had been staged in Europe.

The son of one of the United States' richest men, William K. Vanderbilt Jr. grew up in a world dominated by his father's passion for yachts and racehorses. At age ten, in 1888, he was bitten by the motor bug in the South of France when he rode a steam-powered tricycle seven kilometers from Beaulieu to Monte Carlo. In 1898, shortly after dropping out of Harvard, he had a French De Dion-Bouton three wheeler shipped to him in New York, and the next year he bought his first legitimate car, a Morse roadster from England. Briefly leaving cars aside, as a sailor he won the Sir Thomas Lipton Cup in 1900 but was soon back on land, arrested in Boston for "scorching" through the city in his car and so thoroughly traumatizing the locals in Newport that the city established speed limits—six miles per hour in the center and ten miles per hour elsewhere—just to slow him down. "Arrest me every day if you want to," he was quoted as saying. "It's nothing to pay fines for such sport."

Outside Paris in early 1902, "Willie K." as he was called became the fastest man on Earth when he pushed his Mercedes to 65.79 miles per hour. The next year he raced in a season that included the Circuit des Ardennes (taking third in a Mors) and the aborted Paris–Madrid run; in a stroke of luck, given what happened to some of the other drivers, early on in the ill-fated race he cracked a cylinder of his seven-horsepower Mors. The visit reinforced what he already knew, that American auto manufacturers lagged far behind their European counterparts in ambition and performance. He wanted to do something to motivate his countrymen to think beyond basic utility, to compete with the Europeans in the areas of speed, durability, and quality. Inspired by the success of the Gordon Bennett Cup, Vanderbilt and some friends formed an entity called the National Automobile Racing Association. With time out for Willie K. to travel to Ormond Beach, Florida, near Daytona, to beat Henry Ford's recently set mark and post a new land speed record of 92.30 miles per hour in a new Mercedes, they prevailed in a tough political fight against locals and established the Vanderbilt Cup as the first important American trophy race.

Run on a triangle of dirt roads in Nassau County on Long Island, the event attracted foreign competitors with its large cash prize. But while the crowd on October 8, 1904, was disappointed that an American car didn't win—George Heath, in a Panhard, took the cup—the event scored a major success, and crowds and participation increased enormously over the subsequent two years, with French-made Darracqs winning both times. Unfortunately, at least one spectator—some sources say two—was killed in 1906, triggering a ban the following year. That same year, the first French Grand Prix was run near Le Mans, followed by the initial Targa Florio in Sicily, and in 1907 the Germans followed suit with a major race of their own, the Kaiserpreis; it is this era of pioneering road racing that romantically inclined automotive historians canonize as the Heroic period. Convinced there must be a way to keep serious racing going in the United States, Vanderbilt came up with a solution: He'd build his own course.

At the time, full-blooded auto racers were temperamentally opposed to the idea of specially built, closed-circuit courses; the notion smacked too much of horse racing. Instead, Willie K. decided to personally finance the nation's first stretch of road exclusively designed for the automobile, a proposed forty-five-mile toll road from Great Neck to Lake Ronkonkoma, to be called the Long Island Motor Parkway. Impressively, the first ten miles of it were finished in time for the fall 1908 race, which fittingly served as the occasion for the first American win of the Vanderbilt Cup, by twenty-three-year-old local George Robertson, in a Locomobile. Each year thereafter, the course expanded as construction continued, and the crowds grew along with it until 1910, when four more fatalities, along with numerous injuries, caused New York State to ban road racing altogether. The Vanderbilt Cup moved on to a succession of locations: first Savannah, Georgia, and then Milwaukee, Santa Monica, and San Francisco, but was stopped when the United States entered World War I.

If there was an American equivalent to Camille du Gast, there was only one candidate: Joan Newton Cuneo.

The wife of New York banker Andrew N. Cuneo, Joan bought her first car in 1902 and, after an hour's driving lesson, promptly took her two children for a ride around Central Park. Three years later she was the only woman among thirty-three entrants in the first Glidden Tour, not a race but an event akin to the old French reliability run, a part publicity venture and part social event sponsored by multimillionaire and world traveler Charles Jasper Glidden under the umbrella of the Automobile Association of America and designed to improve automobiles and spread their allure throughout the land, a venture in which he enjoyed particular success with the very wealthy. Mrs. Cuneo, as she was always called, caused a stir on the very first day, during the 121-mile run from New York City to Hartford, Connecticut, when she had to swerve to miss an abruptly stopped car and ended up in a riverbed nine feet below the road, her White Steamer on its side with a bent rear axle and connecting rod, among other ailments. But once the car was put back on its wheels, Joan was able to drive it right out of the river and back to the road. The 870-mile tour ran from July 11 to 22, 1905, traversing roads to Boston and Portsmouth and including a climb up 6288-foot Mount Washington in northern New Hampshire before turning around to head home. Although most locals were enthusiastic and accommodating, some showed their distaste for the horseless carriage by playing pranks such as changing or removing route markers put up ahead of time by the AAA, and cops often took advantage of the participants by catching them in speed traps.

Joan continued to take part annually in the increasingly lengthy and prestigious Glidden Tour, an event that resembled rallying in that it required extremely precise driving to arrive at appointed destinations at an exact minute, with points deducted for failure to do so and for other mistakes. She also began competing successfully against men in amateur races along the East Coast, to the extent that she came to be described in the press as "the most fearless chauffeuse in the world." In her first flat-out timed speed contest in September 1905 she beat three of her four male opponents in an invitational run on the beach at Atlantic City, although she wasn't satisfied with her time for the mile: one minute, eighteen and two-fifths seconds. Her solution was to buy a better car, which she was able to race on a track for the first time at the Dutchess County Fair at Poughkeepsie. "It was a case of love at first sight, and my love for track driving increased each time I drove around one," she confessed. "There was trouble with the oiling system on the car, and my mile exhibition in one minute, twenty-two and one-fifth seconds was a keen disappointment to me. On our drive home the cause of the trouble was found and remedied and we were arrested for speeding." That fall and the following season, Joan won or placed in numerous speed exhibitions, and in 1907, driving against men, she came in third in a grueling one-hundred-mile race at the Bennings track in Washington, D.C.

In early 1909, she flung down the gauntlet by announcing that she would go head-to-head with the nation's top male drivers at the much-anticipated Mardi Gras races at New Orleans in late February. And she would be driving the aptly named Knox "Giant," a fifty-horsepower monster. Joan's participation in the races was heavily ballyhooed, as an American woman had never before taken on men in such an event, where the participants were intent on breaking existing speed records. As the *Los Angeles Times* correspondent put it before the conclave, "There will be no favors after the starting gun is fired, according to those who are in charge of the races, and if Mrs. Cuneo wins it will be on her merits as a driver."

Records began falling with the very first race. Ralph DePalma, one of the top two or three American drivers at that point, broke a track record for one mile in a Fiat Cyclone with a run of 54.2 seconds, while Joan stirred the spectators by setting a women's record in the one-mile with a time of 62.5 seconds, four seconds lower than her personal best. The fifty-miler was a thriller. DePalma won this one too, setting a world mark of 51 minutes, 37.8 seconds. But Joan, making a terrific effort, came in right behind him after a nip-and-tuck battle in which the six thousand-strong crowd cheered as she recovered from a delay for a broken fan belt to overtake George Robertson for second place. Smashing the records of the country's most famous driver, Barney Oldfield, one after another, DePalma also took the ten-mile, setting a new mark in the process. At the end of the day, DePalma announced that he was the best racetrack driver in the world.

The very next day, however, he faltered in the one-mile and one-hundred-mile events, whereas Joan won three races, including the five-mile amateur championship, the ten-mile Klaxton signal race, and a one-mile exhibition. It was a triumphant weekend for her; by so closely challenging Ralph DePalma she had incontestably shown that she could compete with anyone on the circuit. As she put it, "DePalma's specially built track racer was too fast for my car, but I had good cause to be very proud of my records down there." But no sooner had Joan proven herself a great driver than the door was slammed unceremoniously in her face when the AAA abruptly banned women from all further sanctioned racing. That spring, Joan was prevented from competing in several hill climbs and road races, and in August was turned away from the National Stock Chassis competition in Lowell, Massachusetts. Most astonishingly, given her impeccable track record, she was even subject to a general ban on women participating in any way—even as passengers—in that summer's Glidden Tour. In an article entitled "Woman's Automobile Racing Record" in the November 1910 issue of *Country Life*, J. N. Cuneo wrote, "After making these various racing records without accident to myself or others, after driving through the 1908 Glidden tour with a perfect score—which all in the motor world know is one of the most difficult, if not *the most* difficult, of automobile acquirements—I would very much like to challenge any man driver today to show a better record in *all around* driving from the easy few-day touring contests to the beach racing, motordrome contests, hill climbs, road racing, one mile, then halfmile dirt track, and ending with the Glidden tour." But she never got the chance. Just as had happened to Camille du Gast in France five years before, through no fault of her own, Joan Cuneo was forced to stop doing what she loved most and did best.

◻ ◻ ◻

Unfortunate as it was that the wide-open new frontier policies of the nascent sport tightened up as entrenched social attitudes enveloped it, the fact that women were competing at all in the rough and risky realm of auto racing said something about the tectonic shifts taking place in the Western world. As the long Victorian era faded rapidly, the dawn of the new century provided a paradoxical mix of traditional strictures laced with hitherto unthinkable possibilities. Women's suffrage was in the air in many Western countries, although it took years more to implement. Prior to World War I, New Zealand, Australia, Finland, and Norway were the only nations where women could vote; indeed, war seemed required to shake loose these domestic restrictions, for within two years of the end of the Great War in 1918, women had achieved voting rights in more than a dozen countries, including Canada, Germany, Ireland, Poland, the Russian Federation, the United Kingdom, and the United States. It wasn't until after another world war concluded twenty-seven years later that a group of similarly prominent countries, including France, Italy, Japan, Mexico, China, and India, belatedly followed suit.

In the United States, barriers that had stood firm since the birth of the republic began to weaken, if ever so slightly. In 1896, Martha Hughes Cannon of Utah was voted in as the first female state senator, defeating her polygamous husband in the election to do it. The first female police officer was Alice Stebbins Wells, who joined the Los Angeles Police Department in 1910. The

U.S. House of Representatives had a female member for the first time in 1917–19 in the person of pacifist Jeannette Rankin of Montana, and in 1925 Nellie Tayloe Ross of Wyoming became the first woman governor, even if she did replace her governor husband on the ballot when he died just a month before the election.

It was the same in athletics, only different, as women started competing in relatively genteel sports such as golf and tennis in the late 1800s, but against one another rather than with men. Still, by far the most popular sport among women was bicycling; an 1889 all-female six-day race that concluded at Madison Square Garden was an enormous success, and by the end of the 1890s, more than one million American women owned bikes, having bought 25 to 30 percent of all sold during the decade. Leading suffragette Susan B. Anthony declared at the time, "Bicycling has done more to emancipate women than any one thing in the world."

Unsurprisingly, it was well-off women, those most outwardly bound by traditions and social conventions, who, paradoxically, enjoyed the greatest freedom to ignore the rules and thus break new ground in so many fields. This was partly due to their financial advantages, which when it came to cars, boats, and planes, were particularly relevant. It was also the tolerance, even expectation, of eccentricity within the upper class, especially in

Britain but also in the United States. And then there was the sheer confidence of the ruling classes, of the aristocrats in Europe and the wellborn in America, that they could succeed at anything they set their minds to, that there were no limits for them. This was particularly true at first in new endeavors, driving to an extent but especially flying, fields in which there could be no preexisting prohibitions against women's participation.

And then there were journalistic stunts, the prime modern instigator of which was *New York World* reporter Nellie Bly, who made her name in 1887 by pretending to be mad and having herself admitted to the Women's Lunatic Asylum on Blackwell's Island for ten days in order to write an exposé. But by far her most extravagant exploit was her headline-making around-the-world trip undertaken in 1889 in an attempt to beat the fictional mark set by Jules Verne's Phileas Fogg in *Around the World in Eighty Days*. Dreamed up by *World* publisher Joseph Pulitzer as a publicity ploy, the assignment was readily accepted by Bly, whose dispatches were splashed across the paper for the seventy-two days it took her to circle the globe. More sensational coverage was lavished on sixty-three-year-old Annie Taylor, who, in 1901, became the first person to go over Niagara Falls in a barrel and live.

In this light, it isn't surprising that, in the automotive

realm as elsewhere, more attention tended to be paid to "firsts," in the way of extreme endurance or exploits bordering on folly, than to more straightforward competition. The first of these firsts was driving across the United States. Much like the circumstances that launched Phileas Fogg's fictive journey, the long drive of Dr. Horatio Nelson Jackson was instigated by a gentlemen's wager. Visiting San Francisco with his wife, Jackson, a wealthy thirty-one-year-old Vermont physician, bet $50 at the city's University Club that he could cross the country by automobile. No matter that he didn't own a car, and that he and his wife, Berthe, had only recently begun taking driving lessons during their stay in California. A young mechanic named Sewall Crocker agreed to make the trip with him, and suggested he buy one of the strongest cars available, the two-cylinder, twenty-horsepower Winton capable of a top speed of thirty miles per hour. Ironically, the vehicle's manufacturer, Alexander Winton, had only recently failed in his attempt to make the crossing by getting stuck in the Southwestern desert, which helped Jackson decide to take a northerly route roughly following the old Oregon Trail. Having made the bet on May 18, 1903, Jackson spent $3000 on a slightly used Winton, overpaying by at least $500, sent his wife home to wait for him, and set out with Crocker five days later.

Traversing old wagon trails, blowing tires, being pulled out of sand by cowboys, getting sent in wrong directions by untrustworthy locals, crossing rivers by driving over railroad trestles, and generally sleeping under their car, the adventurers labored through the mountainous, little-mapped West. They also acquired unsuspected competition, as two auto manufacturers, Packard and Oldsmobile, scrambled to send out cars of their own in the belief they could overtake and beat them. By the time Jackson and Crocker reached Idaho— where they took on another passenger, a bulldog named Bud—the men were becoming famous. And when they cruised into New York City on July 26 after a trip of sixty-three and a half days, they were received as conquering heroes. But their celebrity was considerably eclipsed five months later when Orville and Wilbur Wright made their short flight in a plane at Kitty Hawk. More men made the trip in Jackson's wake, and within three years L. L. Whitman had whittled the record time for a coast-to-coast trip down to just fifteen days.

More in the category of something that was done just because it seemed like it had to be but that had absolutely no tangible importance whatsoever was the much-bal-lyhooed "Around the World" auto race. Thousands crammed into Times Square on a frigid February 12, 1908, to witness the inauspicious start; only six of the thirteen announced participants actually turned up to undertake the ultimate marathon, sponsored by the French newspaper *Le Matin* along with the *New York Times*. Oriented, like most driving at the time, more toward the makes of cars than the identities of the drivers, the event was laid out to proceed to San Francisco and Seattle, by ship to Valdez, Alaska, across the ice of the Yukon Territory to the Bering Strait, on to Siberia, and hence to the finish in Paris. In the event, the race was both a farce and an almost unimaginably heroic endurance test. Two of the vehicles never made it out of the United States and another expired in Vladivostok—to the undoubted chagrin of *Le Matin*, all the failures were French—and after the Americans arrived in Valdez and found the terrain beyond impassable, it was decided to forego the Alaskan adventure and have the cars shipped directly from Seattle to the Russian port. The American car, a Thomas Flyer, instead ended up in Japan, which it traversed before joining the German Protos and the Italian Zust in Vladivostok. After countless misadventures across Siberia, which had no roads at all, the Protos made it to Paris first, but the Germans were penalized fifteen days for having shipped their car by rail to Seattle after it broke down in Utah. Four days later, on July 30, the Thomas Flyer arrived and was declared champion; George Schuster, who had started the journey as mechanic, had taken over as driver in Wyoming and guided the American car all the way to Paris, racking up 12,116 miles in 170 days, of which 112 were actually spent driving. The Italians brought up the rear on September 17. Unsurprisingly, the contest was never repeated.

In this spirit, the woman who became the most enduringly famous lady driver of America's early automotive days was not a racer but a well-to-do twenty-two-year-old wife and mother from Hackensack, New Jersey, who, in June 1909, set out to become the first woman to drive across the continent. In accomplishing her goal, Alice Ramsey did more than anyone else to put American women behind the wheels of cars.

In 1909, there were just 155,000 automobiles in a country of 80 million people. In the immediate wake of the introduction of Ford's Model T, 290 other car brands competed for the public's attention; manufacturers would try all sorts of promotions to make their names stick in the public mind. One of these companies was Maxwell-Briscoe, and in September 1908, its sales manager, Carl Kelsey, studied Alice Ramsey's performance in her red 1908 Maxwell runabout during the first day of the New York City-to-Montauk Point-and-back reliability run—the only other woman entered was Joan Newton Cuneo—and he liked what he saw. At a dinner that night at the eastern tip of Long Island, Kelsey told Mrs. Ramsey, "You are going to be the first woman ever to drive an automobile across the United States of America, from Hell Gate on the Atlantic to the Golden Gate on the Pacific . . . and in a Maxwell!" No one raised an objection, most important not Alice's husband, John Rathbone Ramsey, a prominent attorney and, at the time, Bergen County clerk who was twenty-three years her senior and never, as Alice put it, "fenced me in." "Bone," as she called him, was entirely disinterested in cars himself, never even learning to drive, but happily indulged his young wife's enthusiasms. Acknowledging that the journey was first and foremost a promotional stunt for Maxwell, Alice was lured by the prospect of "a magnificent adventure" and a challenge that "whetted the appetites of those of us who were convinced that we could drive as well as most men." A self-described "born mechanic" of pert good looks who even in grade school "had elected to take manual training instead of some feminine art," she had left Vassar after her sophomore year in order to marry. Before heading west, Alice squeezed in one more event, the New York-to-Philadelphia round-trip Women's Motoring Club two-day endurance run, in which she and Joan Cuneo were among the nine drivers racking up perfect scores.

Whereas Alice's 1908 Maxwell had a two-cylinder,

fourteen-horsepower engine, the 1909 Maxwell DA with which she was furnished was a four-cylinder job that became popularly known as the "30" thanks to its vastly increased number of horses. A right-hand-drive vehicle with three forward speeds, it was started by a crank affixed to the front, had spark and gasoline throttle levels on the steering column, a glass tube through which oil circulation could be viewed but no gas gauge; the amount of fuel left in the specially enlarged twenty-gallon tank, located under the driver's seat, had to be measured in inches with a wooden stick. Gas headlights allowed for cautious night driving, and extra spare tires were stacked along the running board on the right side, preventing the use of the driver's side door. The car was well built, high off the ground, capable of forty miles per hour, weighed 2100 pounds, and sold for $1500, not quite double the price of a Model T at the time. Without windows even in front, the vehicle was entirely open to the elements, although a retractable faux-leather top provided a measure of relief from rain and intense sunlight.

Alice intended to do all the driving herself and guaranteed this by inviting as her traveling companions three women who didn't even know how. Two were her husband's sisters, Nettie Powell and Margaret Atwood, both in their mid-forties and described by Alice as "conservative and almost haughtily reserved," who had accompanied Alice on the Montauk drive. The other was a robust sixteen-year-old, Hermine Jahns, the sister of a friend, who had proven a lively companion on the Philadelphia trip.

Alice was not the first woman to attempt such a trip. In fact, the first individuals to announce their intention to drive across the country were a married couple, a former army man and newspaper reporter, John D. Davis, and his wife, reporter Louise Hitchcock Davis. Their trip had the backing of the *New York Herald* and *San Francisco Call* newspapers, which were agitating to improve the miserable quality of roads in the United States, a movement that was meeting considerable resistance from the federal government and the railroads. On July 13, 1899, they departed New York City for San Francisco in a National Duryea, a buggylike vehicle with bicycle tires capable of thirty-five miles per hour. From the beginning, it was a journey fraught with mishaps of all kinds. Above all, the car proved unreliable, breaking down so often that, when they were waiting out an eight-day engine-repair delay in Syracuse, they were passed on the road by a one-armed bicyclist who had left Manhattan ten days after they did. Gawkers, of which there were many, felt compelled not only to touch the car but remove pieces of it for souvenirs. The trip, which was originally viewed with enthusiasm by the nascent automotive industry and the press, eventually became an embarrassment, so much so that, after the Davises left Toledo, their trail vanished; some accounts had them arriving in Detroit, others in Chicago. In all events, they were never heard from again.

Another aborted coast-to-coast marathon involving women started in May 1908 when the Idaho-based mother-daughter team of Minerva Miller Teape and Vera Teape McKelvie set out on a proposed two-month journey from Portland, Maine, to Portland, Oregon, in an eight-horsepower Waltham. They made it with relative ease in a little under a month as far as Kansas City, where Minerva, who had health problems to begin with, became severely ill and was packed off to a sanitarium for an extended stay.

It was on the first-ever family trip of its type that women initially came to cross the United States by car. In the summer of the same year, 1908, Jacob M. Murdock of Pennsylvania drove his wife Anna and teenage daughters Florence and Alice to the West Coast. These women were passengers, however, so the opportunity was still open for whatever woman wanted to put her name in the history books by driving coast-to-coast herself.

Still, Alice Ramsey's trip was momentarily upstaged by the highly-touted launch, on June 1, 1909, of the first transcontinental automobile race in the United States, an event whose arrival in Seattle was meant to promote the Alaska–Yukon–Pacific Exposition. William Howard Taft, who three months before had become the first president to ride in a car—a White Steamer—to his inauguration, presided over the start, which proved rather less impressive than intended when only six of the announced thirty-five entrants actually managed to set off. One of the two Model Ts in the race was the first to arrive, on June 23, but was later disqualified when it was discovered that one of the drivers had replaced the engine during the race. Five months after the fact, then, the second car to finish, a Boston-made Shawmut, was declared the winner, and its drivers, H. B. Scott and James Smith, were presented with the Guggenheim Trophy and $2000. The other Model T turned up on June 23, with an Acme following about a week later—by this point, no one was paying much attention. As for the other two, an Itala ultimately arrived in Seattle on a freight car, while a Stears turned out never to have made it out of New York State.

The girl team's 3800-mile journey began on June 9 in pouring rain at 1930 Broadway, the site of Lincoln Center today but then, plausibly enough, the location of Maxwell's Manhattan showroom. Covered by voluminous rubber ponchos, Alice and her companions posed for pictures and answered questions. Reporters were particularly interested in whether or not the women were carrying guns (Horatio Jackson had packed a virtual arsenal on his 1903 foray), and Alice explained that they had been advised not to do so, insisting, "We're not afraid." Although there was no such thing as a national atlas or road guide at the time, A. L. Westgard, known as the "Pathfinder" for his pioneering work in charting automobile routes through the West for the then-five-year-old Automobile Association of America, had advised the voyagers concerning their itinerary, which differed significantly from that pursued by the Seattle-bound racers. Maxwell-Briscoe had also engaged an advance man and press agent, John D. Murphy, automotive editor of the *Boston Herald*, who through much of the trip traveled parallel to the women by train, arranged for their hotels and stirred up local interest.

Escorted as far as Ninety-fifth Street, the women proceeded on their own from there. Fighting pelting rain and roads Alice described as "gluey," they were greeted in Tarrytown by a contingent from Maxwell-Briscoe, as they would be at various burgs across the nation; company representatives had been instructed to help the women out with repairs, tires, and so on whenever necessary. After stopping for lunch in the gloomy shadow of Sing Sing at Ossining, they called it a night in Poughkeepsie, Alice's stomping ground from Vassar days, after chalking up all of seventy-six miles.

What's most fascinating in the account of the trip Alice
Ramsey finally published in 1961, under the title "Veil,
Duster, and Tire Iron," is how primitive conditions
were for getting around the country less than one hundred years ago; west of the Mississippi, especially,
"roads" scarcely merited the name, more often consisting of two weedy ruts across the ground. Cumbersome
chains were required for the slightest inclement conditions. One loses count how many times the ladies'
Maxwell had to be pulled out of mud (they towed others
out as well). Rocks snapped wheels and axles, Indians
and bandits could be a concern (although they were not,
in the end), and accommodations and food in many
towns were barely tolerable. To tide them through, the
ladies subsisted on a supply of bread, butter, and sugar.

And yet an enterprising and resilient tone prevails in
Ramsey's account, which speaks to a persistent optimism
and certainty that the task will be done. Never is there a
complaint about inconvenience, discomfort, or setbacks,
nor an indication of quarrels or fatigue among the travelers, no matter the slowness of their progress. From Albany they headed west, and they were able to cover the
198 miles between Buffalo and Cleveland in one day; Alice was thrilled to be able "to work up the terrific speed
of forty-two miles per hour on the Cleveland Parkway—
our record so far." Parts of Indiana had very good roads

with limestone foundations, but the substantial traffic on them kicked up suffocating clouds of white dust. Around Ligonier, about thirty-five miles southeast of Goshen, the travelers settled onto a route that would, four years hence, become identified as the Lincoln Highway, the first designated coast-to-coast route in the United States. The closer they got to Chicago, the more the women were tossed around by the number of train tracks that increasingly laced the byways.

In the Windy City, they beheld the rarity of an asphalt-paved thoroughfare—fashionable Michigan Avenue had recently been covered by it. The local Maxwell representative invited the women to the Cobe Cup Race in Crown Point, Indiana, an early stock-car racing event won in a Buick by Louis Chevrolet, the Swiss-born future automotive designer whom Alice had met at races in Daytona Beach in 1906.

After a long Chicago weekend, the foursome made their way across the largely gravel roads cutting through Illinois farmland. Pigs frequently dogged their tires, one of which went flat, occasioning a lesson in tire changing, 1909-style, by Alice for the benefit of the local males, who offered to help. But Alice declined on principle, explaining to her companions, "I can't let them do that. I'm supposed to do things like that myself."

This procedure, which she was obliged to repeat

numerous times during the course of the trip, was as laborious and time-consuming as all other aspects of motoring at the time. As she elaborated it, " 'Well, first I raise the wheel off the ground, as you see; then with the pliers I loosen the circular nut at the base of the tire valve stem and remove the tire valve inside. This requires a special little gem of a tool that I always carry in my pocket for safekeeping.' With this remark I reached into said pocket and withdrew the 'little darling.' It was *that*, to me, as it was well-nigh impossible to take out a valve inside without it. 'Now I have to pry off the outside bead of the casing in order to get the tube out.' "

Following numerous further procedures, including the application of tire irons, the manipulation of metal retaining rings, pulling out the old tube, roughing the rubber with a file, applying cement and dusting with talc, Alice agreed to male assistance with the one part of tire changing she hated: pumping it up. The next day they proceeded through mud until they saw a spectacular bridge rising ahead of them, a fourteen-year-old wooden-planked span at Fulton, Illinois, that would take them over the Mississippi and into the West.

A downpour welcomed them to Iowa, producing conditions over the coming days that made Alice "wish we were on Noah's Ark with a real hull under us." They ran out of gas (there were precious few locations to buy it then), were charmed by Indians (the first they had seen) on the Tama Reservation on the way to Marshalltown, and a broken rear axle and dreadful weather made it take thirteen days to negotiate the 360 miles of the "gumbo" that was Iowa.

Nebraska offered more of the same and, at Ogallala, the women with Jersey plates were temporarily detained by uniformed men on horseback who were conducting a murder investigation. Sandy stretches led them into Wyoming, where roads "were scarcely what we would designate as such; they were wagon trails, pure and simple; at times, mere horse trails," Alice noted. "With no signboards and not too many telegraph poles, it was an easy matter to pick up a side trail and find oneself arrived at the wrong destination." Much of the state had been fenced off by ranchers, which meant frequent stops to open and close gates. Two "pilots" guided them across most of the state, but one of them ran his car into a deep ditch. Alice had to come to his rescue, connecting the two cars with rope and tackle, and with everyone else pushing, she pulled out the escort car. To cross the North Platte River, the travelers obtained special permission to use the Union Pacific's railroad trestle. While the others, having traversed the span on foot, waited on the far side, Alice proceeded in the car the only way she could, lining up her left wheels between the two rail tracks while the right wheels moved along outside the right-hand rail, high above the water, and coaxing the car forward in slow, bumpy lurches, the wheels settling each time in the gaps between the wooden ties. While carefully feeding gas and working the clutch, Alice sweated through the three-quarters-of-a-mile ordeal also worrying about the axles and the possibility of a train coming from either direction.

Quickly trying to flee Opal, Wyoming, after sharing a dismal night with bedbugs, kismet arrived in the form of a magnificent new Pierce-Arrow just pulling into town. Two of the three men aboard were Ezra Thompson, former mayor of Salt Lake City, and his son Lynn, just graduated from Yale, and the two parties agreed to drive together to the Mormon capital along twisty but decent mountain roads. Accepting the Thompsons' hospitality when they arrived, the women spent three days in Salt Lake City while their car was restored to top condition, then set out across the desolate terrain for Reno with another "pilot," Sam Sharman, Maxwell-Briscoe's Utah man. Along an innocent-enough-looking dirt road, disaster struck when Alice's two front wheels were splayed at opposing angles by a hidden prairie dog burrow, breaking the tie rod.

There was much worse to come, including an axle collapse, blowouts, carburetor problems, and the endless succession of mountains in Nevada, which was entirely unmarked, resulting in long drives down wrong roads.

The final real test was making it up the steep Sierras out of Carson City. As Alice noted, "The road was heavy with sand. This was in truth no automobile highway. It was an old wagon trail over the mountains and the grades were stiff. Traffic was largely trucking wagons and powerful horses, mules, or even oxen—sometimes just men in the saddle. First a long pull; then rest and cool off at the turn—only to double back up the side of the mountain at a constantly higher altitude." The effort put the Maxwell to the test, but it was more than equal to it. "That sturdy motor had been little short of wonderful in the way it plugged along, day after day, in mud, sand or heat. We simply marveled at it," Alice enthused. Entranced by the sights and lured by an ocean they could practically smell from a couple of hundred miles away, the women all but glided down the mountains and into Oakland, where they drove the Maxwell onto the ferry and crossed over to San Francisco, where, as Alice modestly put it, they were greeted by "a considerable crowd" and "led in a triumphal procession" up Market Street.

The next day, August 8, the *San Francisco Chronicle* headlined its story, PRETTY WOMEN MOTORISTS ARRIVE AFTER TRIP ACROSS THE CONTINENT and, remarking upon

Alice Ramsey's youth and charm, noted that, "She is perhaps the last person in the world that one would expect to find piloting an automobile across the continent with none but three women companions, some hardly older than herself. . . ." Maxwell-Briscoe promoted the crossing's successful completion for all it was worth in ads touting how the model DA had prevailed "over the worst possible roads, over steep grades, and made the trip, one of the most grueling imaginable, without a particle of car trouble." There were, the company insisted, "No mountains or grades too difficult for the Maxwell. No gumbo too thick, no sand too deep for the Maxwell."

Alice quickly returned by train to her family after a two-month absence and settled into domesticity as her husband was elected to the U.S. House of Representatives. Her epic trip, however, inspired Katherine Stokes's trilogy of "Motor Maids" books for girls, about several young women who embark on driving adventures together, published between 1911 and 1914: *The Motor Maids Across the Continent*, *The Motor Maids in Fair Japan*, and *The Motor Maids at Sunrise Camp*. In 1961, more than a half century after the event, Alice Ramsey published her account of the trip, a meticulously annotated version of which was republished in 2005 as *Alice's Drive*. Alice, who died in 1983 at ninety-seven, was also the subject of an illustrated, thirty-two-page book for children, *Alice*

Ramsey's Grand Adventure, by Don Brown, published in 1997.

If Alice Ramsey's coast-to-coast trip was instigated by promotional considerations, some subsequent ventures of its type involving women positively swilled in press agentry and hype. This was certainly true of the next such crossing, by Blanche Stuart Scott of Rochester, New York. Conceived by the Willys-Overland Company to stimulate sales of its cars in particular and attract women to driving in general, the trip was touted from the outset as the first of the country by a woman, a fiction Blanche herself furthered and most of the press, for some reason, bought unquestioningly. In the event, she was definitely the first person to make the journey at least part of the way with an improvised toilet on board, although among the trip's other aims was promoting the idea of a cross-country highway and helping to map a course.

Compared with Ramsey's, Scott's adventure was first-class in every respect. Her car, a four-cylinder, twenty-five-horsepower 1910 Model 38 Overland runabout, was more luxuriously appointed than the slightly more powerful Maxwell had been. She and her companions—Amy Phillips from New York to Toledo, her sister Gertrude from Indianapolis to the Pacific—stayed almost exclusively in swank hotels, enjoyed the benefit of three or four escort cars almost all the way, and were treated to lavish receptions and luncheons in many towns. Among their side trips was a visit to the Indianapolis Motor Speedway, where, in a publicist's dream, Blanche got to meet Barney Oldfield, who let her drive his celebrated Green Dragon. "On the Speedway track I couldn't get it above eighty miles an hour even though not all the horses were going for me," she confessed, adding that, "speed beyond that was too much for me. I wasn't strong enough to hold the wheel on the oblong track. I felt I was somebody. I sailed all that day on Cloud Nine." Blanche and her entourage notched about 5200 miles in their trip's sixty-eight days because they made constant detours to visit as many Willys-Overland dealers in as many cities as possible. So geared toward publicity was the trip of the "Lady Overland" that its traveling press agent, Harry Tuttle, held the ladies back in the East Bay one night so they could arrive by ferry in San Francisco on a Saturday morning, thus facilitating maximum national press coverage in Sunday's papers.

Even in the middle of Wyoming, Scott, a short, no-nonsense woman with an acknowledged big ego, and Phillips were never far from photographers' lenses, which is what prompted them to have their car discreetly installed with a "toidy." This consisted of a hole in the floorboard fitted with a stomach pump equipped with a rubber hose. Once underway again, they were able to drive all day long without stopping, a puzzlement to the gents who wanted to take a break now and then.

Blanche faced some of the same awful road conditions as her unacknowledged predecessor but, compared with Alice Ramsey, she endured remarkably few mechanical problems. Her sponsor was delighted when, in post-run interviews, Blanche declared how much easier the trip was than she had imagined it would be. This no doubt paved the way for two large caravans of cars, which included women and children passengers, that made the national crossing in 1911 and 1912.

This left just one other "first" to be accomplished, that of the first woman to drive solo across the country. This production, not undertaken until 1915, was backed by a major movie studio, no less, and was to star one of its own actresses, Anita King, who had appeared in several important Cecil B. DeMille films: *The Virginian, The Man from Home, Carmen, Chimmie Fadden, The Girl of the Golden West,* and *Temptation.* A native of Chicago, King had appeared onstage with the celebrated Lillian Russell, and studio publicity proclaimed her "the first woman automobile racing driver," allegedly having begun in 1909, although there is no independent record of this; at the most, she may have participated in some local fair races and speed events in Southern California and Arizona. Shortly before her cross-country attempt, she did set the women's speed record for driving from Los Angeles to San Francisco, although this isn't saying much, as her time of nearly eighteen hours paled in comparison to the men's record of twelve hours, ten minutes.

All the same, one of Paramount's three bosses, Jesse Lasky, thought Anita King the woman for the job, and he offered her a strong incentive: If she completed the trip, she would claim the title "The Paramount Girl" and would get to star in her own picture. The studio announced that King would make it to New York in twenty-six days, although, like her predecessor Blanche Stuart Scott, Anita ended up extending what could have been a journey of a little more than 3000 miles into one of 5231 miles for identical promotional reasons—Anita obliged her studio by often driving out of her way to make appearances at 102 Paramount-owned theaters. Unsurprisingly, this resulted in huge nationwide ballyhoo for her undertaking, not hindered by the fact that her car was accompanied—at a discreet distance—front and back by vehicles occupied by Paramount flacks. One can only wonder if Preston Sturges knew about this when he wrote *Sullivan's Travels*, his sublime 1942 film—for Paramount—that includes a hilarious interlude in which Joel McCrea's director takes a motorized adventure from Hollywood into the "real" America, with studio minions at his heels all the way.

The six-cylinder, thirty-one horsepower KisselKar Model 6-52—covered with text saluting King, Lasky, Paramount, the vehicle's manufacturer, and the mayors of Los Angeles, San Francisco, and New York—made its way with much hoopla out of San Francisco on September 1, 1915. Anita had the expected minor problems with the car and the elements, but by now there was an officially designated route to take across the country. The Lincoln Highway eventually became a real road— actually a series of roads—linking the coasts, but at this early stage it was still an idea as much as a highway. After Anita got lost in Nevada and Utah, she noted that the Lincoln Highway could stand better signage.

When Anita King finally reached New York City on October 19, she was escorted by a fleet of about a hundred cars to City Hall, where she was greeted by the mayor, and had a luncheon thrown in her honor at the Knickerbocker Hotel. There were, however, doubts about the legitimacy of her accomplishment. The *Des Moines Register and Leader* disdainfully observed, "Miss King is traveling from San Francisco to New York in her machine, alone. Except for a convoy of four other automobiles loaded to the guards with newspaper reporters, motion picture magnates and magnates' wives and daughters, representatives and employees of tire manufacturing companies, sales agents for automobiles and press agents for motion pictures, she made the trip from Ames to Des Moines alone."

Furthermore, aspects of her trip played in the telling more like a motion-picture scenario, or even a press release, than likely true-life stories, incidents such as being accosted by a hobo who later turned up to offer her flowers, being stalked by a coyote she then shot, and being rescued in the desert by three "prospectors" who found her passed out after she'd gone off course. Finally, cross-country travel by automobile was not nearly as unusual as it had been just a few years previously. Drawn especially by the San Francisco International Exposition, at least six thousand cars made the transcontinental trip or large portions of it in 1915. In the AAA's estimation, it was entirely possible, if not likely, that one or more women made the trip alone with no fanfare during that year.

For Anita King, however, the trip made her more famous than the movies ever did. Lasky lived up to his promise, putting her right into a movie called *The Race*, a comedy-drama about—what else?—a transcontinental car race. According to *Variety*'s review of April 7, 1916, the film was "hopelessly conventional," full of continuity errors and evidence that "The Lasky (Paramount) Company appears to be running out of good scenarios." Only the photography was praised, and King's work went un-mentioned.

Once her film career waned, King took up the inter-esting self-appointed job of advising "star-struck girls," who came to Hollywood with dreams in their heads, about the town's realities and the odds against success, eventually becoming a "City Mother" who lectured far and wide. She also married—into the Carnegie family—gaining wealth and a controlling hand in a stable that pro-duced some fine racehorses.

The final female cross-country voyager worthy of mention before the enterprise became entirely common-place is Amanda Preuss, the first "athlete" among such drivers, who actually trained for the event and, in setting the record for quickest trip from ocean to ocean, so dra-matically reduced the time involved that it merits recog-nition as some kind of sporting accomplishment rather than just a test of nerve, endurance, and mechanical wherewithal. A crack shot and expert angler who, at twenty-five, had been driving for years and could take a car apart and put it back together, Preuss, another Chicago native now residing in California, said that she read of Anita King's drive and thought, "I can beat that and never half try"; her full intention, she said to herself, was "to drive as fast and as far as I could, every day—to set a record." Taking the initiative, she approached

Oldsmobile, a brand she admired, sold them on the idea, and then got additional backing from the YWCA. Her Olds, which she had painted a special battleship gray with discreet lettering on the door identifying the brand, was a sturdy, 26.45-horsepower Model 44 V-8 roadster to which she attached a forward spotlight and extra water pouches. Her intention was "to prove that a capable, self-respecting, well-behaved young woman could go alone from one end of this country to another without molestation or trouble of any sort—for I do hate girls who are always whining about the persecutions of men and the dangers of solitary adventurings."

She trained body and car for six weeks, but two weeks before her departure date she broke her right arm trying to crank start a car. Although she had to take special care, she healed quickly and would not delay her start on August 8, 1916. As she set off from Oakland, what she initially considered a "lark" began to look rather different, as "the seriousness of the thing suddenly came upon me. I realized for the first time what I was really about—that I was facing a venture, success in which meant achievement, approval, honor; and that failure meant disappointment and oblivion. . . . An intense gravity seized me, and from that moment I fought a battle—to win."

The beginnings, across California and the Sierras, and through Nevada, went well. But she was pounded by rain in Wyoming, a state that gave grief to nearly everyone who dared to cross it, and by the time she hit Cheyenne she realized she was falling fifty miles short of her demanding self-imposed goal of three hundred miles per day. Taking a drastic decision, she decided at once to "take the wheel and hang on to it until I dropped, sleep a little and drive until I had to quit again." And so she did, driving the 765 miles from Cheyenne to Ames, Iowa, in forty-one hours, with just six hours off to eat and nap. She slept one night, then promptly motored another four hundred eighty miles, to South Bend, Indiana, in just under twenty-four hours. Once in the East, the going was easier, and when she rolled into Times Square on the afternoon of August 19 (it was her first time in New York City), she had traversed 3520 miles in eleven days, five hours, forty-five minutes, besting her closest female competition by weeks and also, by a mere ninety minutes, edging out the overall record set the year before by motorcyclist Erwin G. "Cannonball" Baker. In doing so, she even beat the daily quota she had established for herself, having averaged a hair over three hundred thirteen miles per day, or close to triple what Anita King had managed.

The significance of these and other attention-getting auto marathons was that they played a strong role in normalizing the idea of women as drivers, to both women and men; provided an antidote to the conventional no-tions of the helpless woman flummoxed by motoring and mechanical challenges; promoted the idea of vacation driving; furthered awareness of the sorry state of American roads, and made conceivable the idea of a solitary woman driving even into the most remote areas of the United States.

But in the years to come, prejudices increased and became more rigid on the racing circuits adjudicated by the AAA. After its ban in 1909, the very year of the opening of the Indianapolis Speedway, women's racing entered the realm of the novelty act, fairgrounds amusement, or patronized opening ornament to actual competition—marginalized in every sense. Closed ovals were built—most had wood-plank tracks, although Indy's was famously changed to brick after its original crushed stone and asphalt surface was partly blamed for the deaths of five people on opening day.

When the United States entered World War I, the AAA suspended all racing, a situation taken advantage of by Ascot Park in Los Angeles when, in 1917 and 1918, it staged a couple of all-female track races. Two drivers emerged from these events as potential stars. One was Ruth Wightman, an eighteen-year-old who already enjoyed a reputation as a flyer and forthrightly announced her ambition to "become the woman Barney Oldfield of the track." The other was Nina Vitagliano Torre, a diminutive Italian native who immediately earned a reputation as a wild one when she lost control in one race and swung around three times before smashing into the guardrails. She later revealed that, because of bouncing and vibrations, she had trouble keeping her foot on the throttle, so she asked her accompanying mechanic—her cousin, as it happened—to put his foot on top of hers to maximize speed.

It was a technique with consequences. Another event was organized for the Speederettes, as the women racers were called, in March 1918, in Stockton, California. The town boasted a large Italian community, which rallied immediately behind Nina Vitagliano Torre when she accepted a challenge from Ruth Wightman to settle the women's dirt-race championship there. Promoter Omar Toft, a well-known racing driver himself, went out of his way to make it a legitimate, first-class event, lining up top-level race cars, adhering to normal AAA regulations, and providing a full briefing on rules, notably the one stressing the dangers of passing on a turn.

A big crowd and plenty of press were on hand for the events of Sunday, March 3. Driving a hulking Stutz No. 8, Vitagliano Torre beat Wightman in the one-mile race, sending the locals into a frenzy. Next up was the five-mile.

Wightman took a small lead through the first lap, but going into a curve on the second lap, Vitagliano Torre tried to pass her on the outside. Then, as the local paper reported it, "The big car was seen to give a mighty leap. It struck one of the pine trees at the middle of the upper turn. There it left the front axle and both wheels. Then it bounded over the embankment, caused by the banked track, hurdled a ditch, crashed through the fence injuring three spectators and finally turned over, a mass of crumpled steel."

Nina Vitagliano Torre was killed instantly; her mechanic, "Bub" Currie, lapsed into a coma to die two days later. Next day, the coroner announced that "the girl's head was driven down into her chest by the terrific impact, her neck being broken in several places and many of the bones of her chest being fractured. She was completely scalped from the eyebrows back."

Ruth Wightman was respectful and dignified in the aftermath, giving the winner's cup to the victim's family and diplomatically suggesting that Nina would have won the race if it had gone the distance. But she also stated, publicly, that, "Miss Vitagliano lost her life by failing to obey the oft-repeated instructions of the race officials." Charitable observers noted possibly inadequate tires on the dead woman's car, a possible blow-out. But others among the press and track crowd suspected that Bub Currie had, at his driver's urging, pressed his foot onto hers to pick up the pace at the wrong time.

After this setback, and with the return of AAA oversight at the end of the war, American women's racing faded back into the margins of sporting life for more than three decades. Some women who raced did so for fun, like the movie stars who buzzed around Douglas Fairbanks' impeccable Beverly Hills racetrack in the very best cars during the 1920s. Others did it for a combination of thrills and a few bucks. These were the barnstormers, who plied a trail from stadium to county fair to "speed carnival" the way stunt flyers and rodeo riders did, driving fast and sometimes agreeing to try evermore outlandish stunts that were often much more dangerous than the regulated racing they were banned from doing for their own protection. It's a testament to the death culture that has surrounded the sport since at least 1903 that one of few women whose name we know from among those countless anonymous daredevils is Elfreida Mais, and we know it only because of the way she died. By 1934, she had been scraping together a living for twenty years on the circuit, where at every town from Wichita to Oklahoma City to Little Rock she was billed as "the world's champion woman race driver." Then one day in Birmingham she announced she would crash her car through a burning wall packed with dynamite. She might have been talked into it for a small bonus, or it could have been her idea. But it was her last run.

OVERSEAS

If you want to be a race car driver, it helps to have money.

—JANET GUTHRIE

I f Britain seems conspicuous by its absence thus far where the birth of automotive competition is concerned, it is because the nation of Victoria had more difficulty than others letting the century of speed begin. At a time when scores of American, French, and other European manufacturers were scrambling to carve a place in the world automobile market, British concerns were stalling and sputtering, with antidiluvian laws preventing road racing from happening at all. But it was from such unpromising beginnings that emerged the most exceptional group of female drivers of the first half of the twentieth century.

As Lord Montagu of Beaulieu, an early British motoring enthusiast, lamented in 1903, "You can beat your wife, steal, get drunk, assault the police and indulge in many other crimes and felonies, and you will find it cheaper than to go at twelve and a half miles an hour." Due to an early-industrial-age law still on the books aimed at large and destructive traction engines, any self-propelled vehicle was limited to a speed of four miles per hour and had to be preceded on the road by a man on foot. As automobiles were viewed scornfully by many, and as a nuisance and a threat by horse-loving country dwellers, early motorists were arrested by local constables for going even five or six miles per hour. A member of Parliament, Lord Montagu pushed for legislation to abolish speed restrictions altogether, and in 1903 a compromise was reached setting a national speed limit of twenty miles per hour. This scarcely improved the country's dire accident and fatalities rate, as the wealthy who began buying fast cars ignored the limit entirely as they tore down city streets and country lanes, knowing police could never catch up with them.

As a by-product of such archaic thinking—Parliament also opposed compulsory-auto-insurance legislation on the grounds that insurance would encourage reckless driving—road racing was simply illegal by virtue of the fact that its very nature compelled speeding; the only events allowed were long-distance trials, hill climbs and short, closed-road speed contests. To participate in any real races, early drivers were forced to travel to Ireland or the Isle of Man.

Under these unlikely circumstances, one English-woman managed to emerge, however briefly, as a star driver, the enigmatic, accidental Dorothy Levitt. At a time when the fastest cars were enormous and required real upper-body strength to steer, this fashion-conscious beauty, whose "Eastern" eyes gave her an exotic look, was plucked from the obscurity of a temporary secretarial position in 1902 at the Napier Motor Company by its managing director, Selwyn Edge, an Australian-born racer who earlier that year had won the Gordon Bennett Cup. Inspired by what Camille du Gast had done for De Dietrichs, Edge figured that, if she could be taught to drive, his tall, stunning protégé could give a publicity boost to his languishing British line. Under his tutelage, she took to it quickly, and within the year won her class in the 1903 Southport Speed Trials driving a Gladiator. The following season she took a silver in the Hereford one-thousand-mile trial, where the annoyance of the otherwise all-male contestants was exacerbated by her unique combination of fancy dress and racing gear, which created a photographic frenzy, and by the little black Pomeranian dog she kept with her at all times; one morning the men all turned up with toy dogs strapped to the fronts of their cars. But in 1905 a new event, the Brighton Motor Week, presented alluring possibilities. Set for July 19–22, the contest would be held Channel-side on Madeira Drive, which had just been freshly resurfaced with a new material called Tarmac. Eager for the rewards of the attendant press scrutiny, Edge deemed Dorothy ready for it and put her behind the huge and barely manageable wheel of the fearsome monster that was the eighty-horsepower Napier works car.

Foreshadowing the official disapproval of female competitors that lay just around the corner, the other drivers treated Dorothy condescendingly, deriding her as a glamorous hood ornament posing no serious threat. Accoutered in trademark duster, cap, and veil, Dorothy thrilled the crowd and surprised everyone with her performance. Two cars at a time were paired for three runs; driving in two classes, Dorothy recorded a lowest speed of 72.52 miles per hour and a high of 78.7, giving her third in one class and first in another, resulting in her startling win of the Autocar Challenge Trophy.

But almost as quickly as her career had accelerated, it stalled and came to a halt. Prevented by Edge from accepting an offer to drive a French Mors in the prestigious Tourist Trophy race on the Isle of Man later that year (one might easily imagine that personal as well as professional issues came into play here), Dorothy competed in hill climbs and enjoyed a measure of success in European events through 1908. Thereafter, she became a demonstration driver for Napier and in 1909 published a book, *The Woman and the Car*, aimed at stirring the interest of potential female drivers. She then vanished from the automotive world and from history, having made a striking if fleeting mark.

It was in reaction to official Britain's harrumphing attitude toward road racing in particular and automobiles in general that the world's first purpose-built racing circuit was born. Disappointed not to have seen any British cars competing in Italy's premiere race, the Targa Florio, in 1906, and fully aware of how badly his country lagged behind the Europeans and the Americans where automotives were concerned, the wealthy landowner Hugh Fortescue Locke King decided what England needed was a proper race course and testing ground. What's more, he would build it. He had the spot for it: three hundred acres of marshy, wooded land that nearly four hundred years earlier had been a favorite hunting ground of King Henry VIII. Just twenty miles southwest of London, with a rail station close by, his property lay along the River Wey, two miles from Weybridge, Surrey. In nine months' time, Locke King enlisted industry support, notably that of Lord Montagu, engaged Colonel Holden of the Royal Engineers to design it, and lodged up to two thousand, mostly Irish, "navvies," who toiled seven days a week.

On June 17, 1907, the Brooklands track was inaugurated. Named after his own estate and designed to seat 30,000 spectators and to accommodate up to 250,000 all around the course, it resembled a bowled amphitheater, featuring a 2.75-mile Outer Circuit that averaged one hundred feet in width and was made of concrete (a forward-looking decision given that concrete was not introduced for public roads until 1912). Its unique signature consisted of two sweeping curved embankments at either end of the oval, the nearly twenty-nine-foot Members' Banking and the roughly twenty-two-foot Byfleet Banking. It was Charles Jarrott, the Paris-Madrid racer who now also worked as an importer of Oldsmobiles from the United States and De Dietrichs from France, who insisted upon the bankings, which would allow high speeds to be maintained all the way around, and Colonel Holden gave assurances that cars could round them safely at up to 120 miles per hour (in the event, numerous cars well exceeded it). During construction, sixteen-hundred-year-old Roman coins and artifacts were uncovered, proving the belief there had been an ancient settlement on the site. At £150,000, the project nearly bankrupted its financier, but it was, in the end, a trendsetting success, inspiring the construction of the Indianapolis Speedway, which opened in 1909, and eventually Montlhery, near Paris, which debuted in 1924, and other European circuits.

Locke King and his wife, Ethel, who went on to do a bit of driving herself, wanted Dorothy Levitt to run in the first Brooklands race, set for July 6, 1907. But the facility's overseers, the Brooklands Automobile Racing Club, whose membership consisted entirely of titled gentlemen, opposed the idea and came up with a splendidly irrefutable excuse not to allow it: As the Jockey Club did not permit female jockeys, there was no reason they had to tolerate female race car drivers. The following summer, officials bent ever so briefly to allow an all-female race decorously dubbed the ladies' Bracelet Handicap, in which the winner, Muriel Thompson, in an Austin "Pobble," barely passed the white flag ahead of Ethel Locke King herself, who in turn was followed by six others (in early Brooklands days, the Union Jack was used to start races and a white one was waved to signal a race's end, the latter replaced by a "chequered" flag around 1930). After a match race that August between Thompson and Christabel Ellis, won by Thompson, the old boys' club put their collective foot down, and no more women raced at Brooklands until after World War I.

The war changed racing enormously, as the technological advances that war inevitably brings bore directly upon the automotive industry. Most crucial was the introduction of stronger and lighter metals. Count Louis Zborowski's famous Chitty-Chitty-Bang-Bangs put powerful aircraft engines into an auto chassis, and in short order came supercharging, the overhead cam, and multivalve engines. Brooklands itself adapted as a result, as the original Outer Circuit with its two huge banks was joined by road-racing circuits that accommodated the smaller, more maneuverable cars that came along in later years.

The even bigger change at Brooklands was its emergence as a center for flying. The first flight of a British-built plane by a British pilot landed on the finishing straight in 1908, and Britain's first aerodrome was soon built at one end of the track. The eminent British aviation firms AVRO, Vickers, Sopwith, and Bleriot all opened factories there. The Royal Flying Corps took over the entire facility during the war, and Locke King's estate remained for many years a busy, noisy center for the fastest forms of transportation on land and in the air.

Its postwar opening delayed until 1920 because of damage the road surfaces had suffered from military vehicles, Brooklands continued to bar women until Hugh Locke King died in 1926 and control passed to his wife, whose pressure forced a change in policy. From 1927 onward, a group of distinctive women racers became a prominent part of the landscape at Brooklands; they were good, too, winning the acceptance of the male drivers and public after all the years of enforced absence.

Sammy Davis, a top driver of the day who won the 24 Hours of Le Mans in 1927, was a colleague of all the Brooklands ladies and entertainingly wrote about them in his book *Atalanta: Women as Racing Drivers*. He perceived very early on how things were and how things ought to be when it came to women drivers: "No sound argument has ever been produced to justify the exclusion of women from races because they are women though smoke screens aplenty have been produced during arguments on the subject.

"The sole yardstick for measurement of skill should be skill not gender, unfortunates who are unable to attain to the necessary standard being ruthlessly removed whatever their sex."

While they were most often segregated to their own ladies' races, at least they got their rides, which is more than can be said for the same period in the United States, and for the best of them it opened the door to some international racing on the continent.

In Brooklands' heyday, beginning in the late 1920s and through the 1930s, there were probably more good women race drivers in England than there ever have been before or since in any given place. The majority, probably, had the advantages of wealth, and several can only be said to be products of the Roaring Twenties, danger-tempting and determined daredevils wanting to live fast but not die young if they could help it; remarkably, most lived into their eighties and nineties. A trailblazer among them, if not also the most headstrong dilettante, raced under the ultra-traditional *nom de vitesse* of the Hon. Mrs. Victor Bruce. This was, in fact, Mildred Mary Petre, the only daughter among six privileged children who proved to be a triple threat, madly pursuing early records in race cars, speedboats, and most famously, airplanes.

Marrying Victor Austin Bruce, grandson of the second Lord Aberdare, at age thirty in 1926, she started in the first women's event at Brooklands since the war, in June 1927. Scoffing at the formless overalls customarily worn by women drivers, Mildred flaunted elegant cocktail wear at the track. She jumped into any automotive event that struck her mad fancy, with an eye toward setting attention-getting records. With her husband as passenger, she drove through Scandinavia to where the road simply stopped, 270 miles north of the Arctic Circle, planting a British flag in the snow at the spot. In similarly frigid temperatures, Mildred and Victor set numerous records by driving 15,000 miles over ten continuous days and nights at Montlhery, and in 1929 Mildred put her name in the books again with a twenty-four-hour Montlhery marathon at an average of 89.4 miles per hour that represented the longest uninterrupted solo drive on record.

Not content limiting herself to cars, Mildred that same year set records in her speedboat for time across the English Channel, both for a single crossing and for the Dover–Calais round-trip, which she managed in seventy-nine minutes. She then matched her automotive endurance mark with her motorboat, driving it for an unprecedented twenty-four hours.

From here, there was nowhere to go but up—in the air. Strongly foreshadowing the heroine of Gilbert Frankau's 1932 novel *Christopher Strong* (and the Dorothy Arzner film starring Katharine Hepburn that arrived a year later), Mildred followed her earthbound exploits by purchasing a plane and announcing her intention to circumnavigate the globe alone, this just three years after Charles Lindbergh's first solo flight from New York to Paris. With just forty hours of solo flying behind her, Mildred set off from England and made it as far as Japan, although it took her two months to do so thanks to one crash, a forced landing, and other mishaps. However erratic her progress, she still became the first person to fly from London to Tokyo, and in the process set the record for longest solo flight to that time. She piloted a plane for the last time at age eighty-one and died peacefully at ninety-four.

Another woman known more as a speed queen than for driving finesse was, to give a full account of her frequently expanding name, Gwenda Glubb Janson Stewart Hawkes. The daughter of a highly decorated major general and sister of "Glubb Pasha," the celebrated commander of the Arab Legion—both knights of the realm—Gwenda Glubb learned to handle vehicles on the worst terrain and under fire as an ambulance driver on the Russian and Romanian fronts during World War I. As a competitor, motorcycles were her first enthusiasm, and by 1922 she had set several endurance records, including a "Double Twelve Hour," for two wheelers at Brooklands in private events. Restrictions at the English circuit prompted Gwenda and her second husband, Colonel Neil Stewart, a racing-world insider, to move to Paris, where they not only set up shop at the Montlhery track but even lived there, creating cozy quarters in the girders under the high banking "much as a bird's nest is constructed in a tree," as fellow British racer Sammy Davis put it. Gwenda, who, with her brushed-back short hair, high forehead and partiality to trousers and collared shirts, was the most mannish looking of the women drivers, was to all appearances unafraid and unbothered by the monotony of near-endless repetition. So many motorcycle speed and endurance marks did she set at the French track that she became known locally as the Queen of Records, and she was decorated by the French government for her efforts. A fine mechanic, she shortly graduated to a three-wheeled Morgan designed for her by engineer Douglas Hawkes, with whom she commenced a little-concealed affair and whom she eventually married; in the three wheeler, an odd-looking beast that resembled an oblong egg, she set a speed record of 115 miles per hour that was never surpassed.

To facilitate Gwenda's inevitable transition to four-wheeled vehicles, Douglas Hawkes bought her an Indy car, the speedy Miller Special, which he made even more powerful at his family's Derby Motor Company. The result was the front-wheel drive Derby-Miller, commonly known as the Derby Special, a high-strung but blindingly fast rocket in which Gwenda was able to set numerous records at Montlhery, including those for average lap speed of 140 miles per hour and for top speed, first of 145.94 miles per hour and finally 149, an outright record for men and women that stood unequalled until after World War II.

That said, Gwenda never became a successful racing driver per se, always preferring record breaking because, as she bluntly put it, "It required no driving skill." Gwenda geared herself toward speed and endurance from the outset because she saw that women were not restricted in those realms; a record is a record, regardless of sex or anything else. But because others insisted she was too good not to try real racing, she gave it a whirl. Beset by doubts, she washed out in assorted European races, including Le Mans, whereupon she and Douglas returned to England, a challenge awaiting her: a match race between her and local favorite Kay Petre to crown "The Brooklands Speed Queen."

Fans packed in to witness the heavily promoted contest on August 3, 1935, as it promised to be a fantastic battle. Officials started sweating when the women exceeded 130 miles per hour in practice, a rarified milestone only sixteen drivers of either sex would ever achieve during the twenty-eight seasons of Brooklands. Afraid that Gwenda and Kay would fight to take the tops of the bankings in order to maintain speed—with possibly disastrous results—the authorities persuaded the ladies to drive three laps separately, with the title to go to the woman with the single fastest lap. Kay, in a 1924 10.7 litre Delage, went first, making her best run the second time, at 134.24 miles per hour. In her 1.6-liter supercharged Derby Special, Gwenda hit 133.67 on her first try, but then had to turn in when the silencer she was forced to install exploded. Officially, then, Kay won the challenge, but Gwenda had the final say the next day when she took her car out again and ran a lap at 135.95 miles per hour, a speed no woman at Brooklands ever topped.

Moving into Brooklands much as they had lived at Montlhery, the Hawkeses ran the Brooklands Engineering Company through the war and in later years sailed the Mediterranean on their small yacht, the *Elpis*. Like Mildred Bruce, Gwenda, who thrived on living dangerously, survived into her dotage, dying at ninety-five.

Once Brooklands opened up to female drivers once and for all in 1927, women became a permanent, welcome, and popular part of the scene at the circuit and, therefore, in England. In no other country, even in France and Italy—where the occasional *femme rapide* had been an accepted part of the sport from the beginning—were women so numerous or successful in the twelve years leading up to World War II as they were in Great Britain. Granted, there were limitations. At first, they were largely restricted to private club meetings held at Brooklands, and later to separate ladies' races organized by the Junior Car Club. But there were some occasions when the women were able to compete against men, and several of them, especially those who earned the rare 130 miles per hour badge, proved they possessed the skill Sammy Davis insisted should be the only requirement for racing.

Along with Mildred Bruce and the winner, M. J. Maconochie, another woman who ran in that first Brooklands women's event was Jill Scott. Wealthy to begin with, she became more so by marrying William Berkeley

"Bummer" Scott, a Scotsman and early motorcyclist who started his auto racing career at Montlhery in 1924 and bought cars for himself and his wife as if they were changes of clothes. They frequently raced together, recording dozens of wins at Brooklands through the end of the 1920s. Like Gwenda Hawkes, Jill was a lead-footed speed demon, becoming the first woman to join Brooklands' exclusive 120-mile-per-hour club when she reached the milestone on a lap in 1928. She took up flying and, in 1929, left Bummer to marry Ernest Thomas, a pilot with whom she raced at Brooklands in the late 1930s.

Another upper-class rose, Violet Cordery, was known as "The Long-Distance Lady" for her extraordinary endurance runs. In 1926, at age twenty-five, she became the first woman to win the Royal Automobile Club's Dewar Trophy, awarded for an impressive string of record-setting distance drives: the ten-thousand-mile Monza race, a subsequent fifteen thousand-mile event, also in Italy, and a five-thousand-mile marathon on the track at Montlhery at an average speed of 70.7 miles per hour, all accomplished in a three-liter Invicta. The following year, Violet circumnavigated the globe in another Invicta, taking five months to drive through Europe, Africa, Asia, Australia, and North America in the company of a mechanic, nurse, and an RAC observer; there were remarkably few mishaps. Violet's husband, Johnny Hindmarsh, was also a racer as well as a pilot, winning at Le Mans with Luis Fontes in 1935, although he died in a crash flying out of Brooklands in 1938.

There were other notable British women drivers during this period: hill-climb ace Eileen Ellison, a sparkling blonde who scored her greatest victory in 1932 when she won the Duchess of York's race at Brooklands in her Bugatti against top competitors Elsie Wisdom, Kay Petre, and Fay Taylour; well-to-do Scotswoman and big-car specialist Margaret Allan, one of four women to earn a place in Brooklands' 120-mile-per-hour club, member of the all-female MG team that did so well at Le Mans in 1934, and after World War II, automotive columnist for *Vogue*; the slim, ultra-disciplined MG driver Dorothy Stanley-Turner—from a wealthy and distinguished military family—who finished sixteenth with Joan Riddell at Le Mans in 1937, and won both the first Easter Road Handicap in 1937 and the last race run at Brooklands, in 1939; and the deceptively frail-looking Doreen Evans, who, with her two older brothers, practically grew up at Brooklands, first raced at seventeen, had considerable success there, and, along with Margaret Allan, Colleen Eaton, Barbara Skinner, Joan Richmond, and Mrs. Gordon Simpson, was part of Captain G. E. T. Eyston's MG works team that impressed at Le Mans in 1935.

There had been successful husband-and-wife racing teams in England in the 1920s, perhaps most notably Bill and Ruth Urquhart Dykes, who set a twelve-hour speed record at Brooklands of 81.38 miles per hour in 1928. On her own, Ruth won several Brooklands women's races and in 1927 became the first woman to finish the gruelling three-hundred-mile road race at the Boulogne Speed Week. But the standout racing couple of the 1930s was unquestionably Tommy and Elsie Wisdom, with the even-tempered, efficient Elsie soon eclipsing her journalist/ gentleman-driver husband, nicknamed "Tinker," as the more talented of the pair. As Sammy Davis observed, "husband and wife do not usually make the best partners as racing drivers but these two did," based on their similar approaches to driving, a healthy frankness, and complementary senses of humor. Like Gwenda Hawkes, a motorcyclist first, Elsie, who was commonly called "Bill," easily won her first Brooklands race, the Ladies' March Handicap, in 1930. The following year she earned the coveted 120-miles-per-hour badge. Then, having proven she could hold her own against top male competition, she entered one of the biggest events of 1932, Brooklands' first-ever thousand-mile race. Held across two days (neighbors had successfully petitioned to eliminate night racing at the circuit, thus banishing twenty-four-hour events), the contest paired Elsie in a Riley 9 with Joan Richmond, a fine

Australian racer who had recently traveled all the way to England by car, with a stop for the Monte Carlo Rally on the way. By averaging eighty-five miles per hour throughout the twelve hours, the duo ended the first day in fourth place in the 1000cc class, very close behind the first three cars. Despite tie rod and tire problems, they were able to maintain the pace the next day and finished first, three minutes ahead of many top male drivers and works teams.

Elsie's triumph earned her one of the six slots on the Aston Martin team preparing for the Rudge Cup race at the 1933 Le Mans, where she teamed with Le Mans regular Mort Morris-Goodall; they ran very well until engine trouble forced them to retire from the race. That same year, Elsie was the only woman entered in the International Trophy race at Brooklands, and in finishing an impressive third was one of only eight of twenty-eight starters to finish. In a lap record competition at Brooklands in 1934, Elsie set a new women's speed record of 126.73 miles per hour at Brooklands.

Invited twice more to race at Le Mans, Elsie had a setback in 1937 when she and Tommy drove an MG together in Italy's Mille Miglia, a perilous thousand-mile annual ritual run on public roads. The contestants set off from Brescia in the north and moved on in a clockwise direction to Verona, Ancona, and Pescara on the Adriatic,

across to Rome, then north through Siena, Florence, and
Bologna, cut up to Piacenza and reversed back east to
Mantua before returning to Brescia. It was a lingering
vestige of racing's earliest city-to-city marathons, complete with obsessed locals pressing in along the roads to
observe the action from a little too close-up, or just citizens going about their business. It was the latter that did
Elsie in, as Tommy, swerving to avoid hitting a woman,
ran into a tree, and then another, sending his wife flying
from the passenger seat through the windshield and
into a long convalescence involving a good deal of plas-
tic surgery. Still, she came back, running at Le Mans yet
again in 1938 before turning to motorboat racing and, after the war, appearing at rallies and hill climbs, sometimes with her husband and other times not.

Very likely the most popular—and in many people's
minds the best—lady racer to call Brooklands home during the 1930s was Kay Petre. A pretty diminutive brunette
at four feet ten, Kathleen Coad Defries was the daughter
of a wealthy Toronto barrister with strong British connections. In Canada she met a visiting young London solici-
tor and amateur pilot, Henry Petre. They went to England,
married, and then he introduced her to the Brooklands
crowd—much to their surprise, in that his hitherto total
avoidance of women had earned him the nickname "Peter the Monk." Henry bought her a Wolseley Hornet Day-

tona Special, in which she was tutored in driving on the Brooklands track by some accommodating professionals.

Called a "young sprite" by lifelong friend Sammy Davis, Kay took to the limelight from the outset, winning numerous women's races, always appearing in a tailor-made white leather jacket and matching helmet and invariably pausing at the end of a race to freshen her makeup before presenting herself to photographers; her popularity with them got her picture splashed across more newspapers than any other woman racer. She was often loaned good cars by other drivers, although because of her stature, she could only reach the pedals after she had a custom-made seat fitted that could be fastened into their cockpits. It was her husband's pleasure to buy her new cars on occasion, and she was able to move up to an Invicta, a Bugatti, and in 1934, the ex-Cobb 10.5-liter Delage, a difficult-to-handle behemoth that to everyone's amazement she was able to drive, much less set a women's Outer Circle lap record of 129.58 miles per hour.

In June 1934, Kay and her partner, Dorothy Champney, were among the group who became the first British women to complete the world's most famous endurance race, the 24 Hours of Le Mans, finishing a very impressive thirteenth in Champney's Riley 9 Ulster Imp out of a field of forty-four entrants, among them Gwenda

Hawkes (teamed with Frenchman Louis Bonne) in her Derby L8, who did not finish. The following season saw the highly publicized "Brooklands Speed Queen" face-off with Gwenda Hawkes, which Kay won, and then lost. She continued to drive in numerous international events, including the 1937 South African Grand Prix, coming in eleventh, and later that year reached the pinnacle of her career when she became the only female member of the hallowed Austin works team and received an unusual 750cc side-valve model. Kay drove solidly at numerous events in Britain and France through the summer, but in September her racing career came to an untimely end. Throughout its history, Brooklands was the scene of comparatively few fatal crashes and major catastrophes. And in more than one hundred years of automobile racing, very few of the women involved in the sport have had serious wrecks or been badly hurt. Elsie Wisdom's Mille Miglia injuries were bad enough, but Kay Petre's were much worse—and in neither case were as a result of any fault of their own.

During practice for a five-hundred-mile Brooklands race in September 1937, Reg Parnell's MG stalled near the top of the Byfleet banking, slid down the curve nose first, clipped the rear of Kay's Austin as it sped along the inside, and sent it tumbling all the way to the bottom. Suffering from terrible head injuries, Kay clung by a thread for several days and eventually pulled through, although she needed numerous operations and her face was henceforth partially paralyzed. Parnell was found guilty of causing the accident and had his license temporarily revoked. Kay returned to the track, in March 1938, for one run. This was enough to tell her she'd lost something she could never get back, and she quit, so demoralized that she refused to discuss either the accident or racing for a considerable time. Eventually, she started rallying and writing about cars for newspapers. Her husband died in 1962, while Kay lived another thirty-two years, passing away at ninety-one.

A star driver of a rather different order, and ultimately both the most colorful and controversial female driver of her or any time, was Fay Taylour. Well raised and educated in an affluent Irish family, she learned to drive at twelve and became hooked on motorcycles while at Alexandra College in Dublin. In fact, for women to take up motorcycling was not all that unusual. Initially it was seen as an adventurous extension of bicycling, which was very popular among women. At its peak, there were roughly 25,000 female motorcyclists in Great Britain, although the number declined for both men and women thereafter. Fay followed her fancy to England, where she first raced on dirt and grass tracks, and was accepted as the real thing from the moment in 1927 when she beat all but one of the male riders in the Camberley Club dirt track contest. She shortly graduated to the helter-skelter world of speedway racing, where her ferocious, unrestrained style made her a big hit in the cavernous halls and stadiums where it was held. The yelling of the crowds in these places could never compete with the noise of the bikes, which created a deafening din. Curiously, women constituted a noticeably higher percentage of the attendance at speedway racing than at any other sporting events in Britain. One spectator who saw Fay at London's Crystal Palace in 1928 reported, "She broadsided round the corners and was winning easily when, through being over-cautious at the last bend, fell off, turned a couple of somersaults, jumped up, grappled with the motor and with the help of Charlie Datson jumped on again and rode in over the line to the cheering of twenty thousand people." Because there was just one other strong female motorcyclist at the time, "Fay Taylour versus Eva Asquith" became a huge attraction at circuits all over Great Britain, to the considerable profit of the "enemies."

Fay represented the British Isles quite handily on a tour of Australia and New Zealand in 1929–30, more often than not besting local champions wherever she raced. After a speedway racer named Vera Hole broke her collarbone in England in 1930, authorities banned women from motorcycle competition. Fay turned to four-wheeled vehicles and quickly moved into the upper ranks, taking the 1931 Brooklands Women's Handicap in a Talbot 105 and coming in second in the same event the following year with a 113.97 miles-per-hour lap time in a Monza Alfa Romeo. Because of her extensive motorcycling, she was especially good on dirt. In an incident that helped cement her reputation as a wild thing, after the end of a 1932 Brooklands race, "Flying Fay from Dublin" kept on lapping the Outer Circuit at a tremendous speed, refusing to stop. When she finally pulled in, she was laughing about the whole thing. But officials didn't find it so funny, disqualifying her and slapping a fine on to boot. After observing her in action, Sammy Davis cogently observed that she "drove with skill, violence, and an occasional disregard of regulations."

Beating a diplomatic retreat by returning to her native land for a spell, she was the only woman entered in the 1934 race for the Leinster Trophy, and won it. More than any of the other women of the era, she raced everywhere—the Mille Miglia, in Scandinavia, in the 1938 South African Grand Prix, even in the United States, where she was called "Lady Leadfoot." A big partier with a motor mouth, she wasn't much liked by her fellow drivers and preferred socializing with the upper crust, racing officials, power brokers, and politicians, which is how she got into trouble.

In the late 1930s, Fay became enamored of far-right leader Oswald Mosley, joining his British Union of Fascists and a particularly insidious organization called the Right Club. After World War II began, Fay came to be viewed as a threat by British intelligence and was interned from 1940 to 1943, mostly on the Isle of Man. Files declassified by MI5 reveal that, in one letter, Fay wrote, "I love Nazi Germany and the German people and their leader and this war seems terribly unfair." She was mysteriously released with the agreement that she would leave Britain and remain in Ireland, but concerns lingered within the government, with one report noting that Fay Taylour was ". . . one of the worst pro-Nazis in Port Erin . . . She is in the habit of hoarding pictures of Hitler and had in her possession a hymn in which his name was substituted for God's."

Despite all this, Fay was among the few women drivers from the prewar era who resumed her career after 1945; for her, racing was all. She never married and, for quite a few years, was able to continue her peripatetic ways, returning to Australia for very successful appearances and, by the late 1940s, landing in Los Angeles, where she became a salesperson at Roger Barlow's International Motors. She also competed at two of the earliest sports car races held in Southern California. Sanctioned by an ad hoc organization called the Foreign Car Racing

Association, the events were held in the summer of 1949 at Carrell Speedway in Gardena, where the half-mile banked dirt oval made Fay feel right at home. On July 24, she drove an MG TC to a second-place finish, behind Jack Early, in a three-lap match race, an event she won when it was repeated on August 21. Future luminaries Phil Hill, John von Neumann, and Al Moss also drove in these preliminaries to the great decade to come. Fay later jumped into midget car racing and occasionally found rides at major circuits against the new generation of star drivers. She finally retired to Dorset in the late 1950s and died in 1983. In a 2003 assessment of her exceptionally eventful life, the *Irish Times* noted that the issue of her former political sympathies and resultant detention had been "airbrushed out of all her publicity."

The Continent, and particularly France, had its share of outstanding women drivers between the wars, and they had more opportunities to race against men than did the Brooklands group. If one woman's name comes up more than any other in estimations of the best female racing driver of them all, it's Eliska Junek. Her career was relatively brief—about five years, perhaps just the last two at top form—but this petite, intensely dedicated Czech remains the only woman to have won a Grand Prix event. She was eventually accepted as an equal by the men who might have initially scorned her; Stirling

Moss later observed that among women drivers, "only Junek could worry top men drivers in *grand prix* cars." Born Alzbita Junkova in Moravia, she always preferred to be called Eliska, was nicknamed "Smisek" due to her quick smile and became known as Elizabeth when her career went international. A linguist—she knew German, English, and French in addition to her native tongue—at sixteen she got a job in a bank, where she met rising banker Vincenc "Cenek" Junek, seven years her senior. Their courtship was an on-and-off, tempestuous thing interrupted by her wanderlust. But she did come to share his love of cars, and after they married in 1922 and he bought a Bugatti 30, a memorably cigar-shaped craft, Eliska began riding with him as mechanic in local races. However, an old wound of Cenek's sometimes made gear shifting difficult—he'd been shot in the hand during World War I—so his wife got behind the wheel and stayed there, becoming a local celebrity when she won the Plzen-Tremosna hill climb in 1924. In 1925, after Europe followed the United States' lead in barring riding mechanics, the couple bought another Bugatti, and the following spring, Eliska took it to Sicily to drive in the world's toughest race, the Targa Florio.

She and Cenek arrived a month early, determined to learn the road in minute detail to get a leg up on her mostly Italian competitors, who generally just gave the course a casual spin-around prior to the big event. Physical strength counted for more in the Targa Florio than in any other race; at this point the course, which was altered periodically through the years, ran sixty-seven miles (to be repeated five times during the race) through very wild country dominated by rugged mountains, an estimated one thousand hairpin turns, steep drop-offs from the edge of the rocky, dusty roads, and medieval villages that were home to citizens not always known for their welcoming embrace of outsiders. Driving the Targa consisted of constant hard work of forever turning to make sharp turns at the highest possible speed on uncertain surfaces, topped off by uninterrupted vigilance. Aware she'd have to gain an advantage by some means other than brute strength, Eliska became one of the first drivers to do what later became common practice: Accompanied by her husband, she walked most of the course, observing the lay of the road and determining the best line through corners and turns.

Up against twenty-three male pilots when the race began, she was running fourth when her steering gave out and she had a smashup, precariously near a cliff. Despite this, she received great respect for her showing and was given a special trophy for heroic driving. In July, she solidified her status as a top competitor—regardless of sex—when she won in the two-liter class at the rigorous

Nürburgring in Germany, making her the first—and still only—woman to win any Grand Prix event (granted that the Grand Prix designation didn't then mean what it does today, in that essentially any location could at that time deem its racing event a Grand Prix).

In 1928, Eliska was ready to attempt the Targa Florio again, this time in a new black-and-yellow Bugatti 35B the equal of anything the men would be driving. And this year, lo and behold, there was one other woman among the contestants, the Countess Einsiedel, arrived from Germany with a 1500cc Bugatti. After one lap Eliska was fourth behind the great Monagasque driver Louis Chiron, also in a Bugatti. During the second lap, she passed him, then caught sight of the leader, Albert Divo. Little by little, she crept up, and for three full laps it was a mad contest in which both drivers pushed their cars to the limits, with Eliska nipping at Divo's heels for a good 270 miles. Sammy Davis, who was an eyewitness, reported that Divo was finally able to pull away on the fifth lap. More commonly asserted lore has it that, on the final lap, Eliska and Giuseppe Campari were in a close battle when she suddenly saw two large rocks in the road that hadn't been there before. She was forced to swerve and stop, and before she or Campari could get started again, Divo slipped past them to victory. In the event, Eliska finished in fifth place, still ahead of twenty-five others, but there were insinuations that the rocks had been placed there to prevent a foreigner—and a woman, no less—from winning; it had been a blow in 1924 when the German Christian Werner became the first non-Italian to capture the Targa Florio. He was to remain so for fifty years.

Eliska shortly returned to Nürburgring, this time to drive with her husband. It was July 15, and she had just handed the car over to him when it went off the road and Cenek was killed when his head struck a rock; he was thirty-four, she twenty-seven. Utterly bereft, Eliska quit racing forever and immediately sold their cars. In a macabre irony, the Bugatti 35B Cenek had been driving was little damaged and was bought by Czech racer Josef Harak, who, on September 29 in the Ecce Homo hill climb, crashed it into a tree and died, thereby endowing that Bugatti with the dark reputation of the car that killed twice. Eliska much later remarried but remained in Prague, where the postwar communist government, disapproving of her former high-flying lifestyle as the famous "Queen of the Steering Wheel," stripped her of all status and prevented her from traveling for many years. In postwar racing circles, the story circulated that she had been spotted laboring unhappily in a tire factory. In very old age she reemerged somewhat, attending at least one automotive gathering in Great Britain and even, at ninety-one and against doctors' orders, flying to the United

States for a Bugatti event in 1989. She died five years later. Looking back, she said, "I proved that a woman can work her way up to the same level as the best of men. We women sometimes tend to blame our failures on nature. It is far more productive to be less angry and more hardworking. Some handicaps can easily be overcome."

France produced several prominent lady drivers in the 1930s; coincidentally or not, they all happened to be petite and notably pretty. Most stuck with rallying, but a few went further. The first women to enter the 24 Hours of Le Mans, in 1930, were Marguerite Mareuse and Odette Siko in the former's Bugatti T40, and they finished a remarkable seventh overall. The following year, the pair were disqualified for refueling too early. Siko returned in 1932 and this time, paired with Louis Charaval (racing under the name Jean Sabipa), she finished first in the two-liter, 1501–2000cc class and fourth overall in her Alfa Romeo 6C 1750, which was evidently the first Scuderia Ferrari car ever to show up on the circuit. This remains the best showing ever for a woman at Le Mans. The next year, in the same car, she was lucky to survive a bad crash in the event, and she never returned.

The most frequent female driver at Le Mans in the prewar years was Anne-Cecile Rose-Itier, more commonly known as Anne Itier, who competed there five times in a row through 1939. A spirited redhead who, it was speculated, escaped into racing in reaction to an unhappy marriage to a Scotsman, she flew planes first, and then spent three years in rallies and hill climbs until she switched to racing Bugattis in the early 1930s. She appeared in some Grand Prix races and had a reasonable record at Le Mans, finishing thirteenth and fourteenth paired with men in 1934 and 1935. French political turmoil knocked out the 1936 race, and Anne failed to finish in 1937 when she teamed with the German Huschke von Hanstein, with whom she had started a big romance after he "rescued" her when she got lost in the desert during the Morocco rally earlier in the year. She recouped in 1938, coming in twelfth, and suffered an accident when racing with Suzanne Largeot, herself a three-time Le Mans participant, in 1939. Four women made unremarkable runs at Le Mans from 1949 to 1951. Then, in a telling illustration of how things had changed in Europe for women after the war, it was silence for twenty years; the eminently qualified American speedster Denise McCluggage and the fine Irish driver Rosemary Smith were refused by Le Mans, which barred women's participation entirely after the accident-prone Annie Bousquet was killed at the 12 Heures de Reims in her Porsche in June 1956. Finally, in 1971, Marie-Claude Beaumont was able to begin her run of six straight appearances there and, more impressively, Anny-Charlotte Verney

TODD MCCARTHY

chalked ten consecutive, and mostly strong, showings from 1974.

And then there was Helle Nice, one of the most famous between-the-wars female drivers who declined into desperate anonymity, only to return posthumously to the spotlight she so adored via Miranda Seymour's rich, if necessarily somewhat speculative 2004 biography, *The Bugatti Queen*. Nice, nee Helene Delangle, emerges from its pages, if not necessarily the greatest of women *pilottes* then certainly the raciest, in both senses of the word. She won races, and was for a time the fastest woman in the world by stopwatch. She was also sensationally promiscuous, evidently readily sleeping with anyone who might advance her career, loan her a car, help her out, or none of the above.

A village girl born in 1900, she became a nude postcard model and dancer in Paris, and through show business circles met auto-world figures who got her into cars. In June 1929, she came out of almost nowhere in her white overalls and cap to win the first Grand Prix Feminin in an Omega-Six at Montlhery. Six months later at the same track on a frigid day in December and after entering the realm of Ettore Bugatti, she set a world speed record of 197.708 kilometers per hour and an average speed of 194.266 across ten miles.

For a few years, the world was hers. She raced the best

110

new Bugattis; did a demonstration tour up and down the East Coast of the United States, where she was dubbed "The Speedbowl Queen"; appeared in advertisements on both sides of the Atlantic; raced in Grand Prix and competed against the top male drivers; won the Monte Carlo Ladies' Cup in January 1935 with the Russian Madame Marinovitch by driving four thousand kilometers from Tallinn to Monaco in the dead of winter, and slept with everyone from her mechanics to the Baron Philippe de Rothschild.

Then, as she was looking to move into the lead of the São Paulo Grand Prix in July 1936, a bale of hay somehow materialized in the middle of the road as she swung around the curve into the final stretch. When she hit it at 93.21 miles per hour, she sailed out of the car, collided with a spectator, splitting his head open, while her car careened into people jammed behind the barrier along the road. Six were killed and about three dozen were rushed to the hospital, where Helle Nice lay in a coma for three days. It was the worst racing accident on record in South America. Three months later she was able to return to France, but this was the end of her international career. She did set some more records with an all-female Yacco team and won a major women's race three weeks before World War II started. But her luck was spent, especially after the war when she was accused by Louis Chiron of having collaborated with the Nazis, a charge that remains impossible either to prove or discount. An accident put a virtual halt to her halfhearted comeback in the Monte Carlo Rally of 1949. She lived, in increasing squalor in Nice, until 1984.

Many of the women drivers—most of the British, probably, and some of the French, including Itier—were content enough with ladies' races. Like Eliska Junek, however, Helle Nice wanted to prove that she belonged on the same track with any man, and sometimes she did. Still, there are skeptics, among them Denise McCluggage, who feel that Helle Nice was, more than anything, a self-absorbed spotlight queen, "like a bear on rollerskates. The question is, Who did she beat? The answer is, she never beat anybody of any stature on a regular basis in any races that mattered. But Madame Junek, she was a serious driver with a terrific knack. She was a great driver."

World War II created a long interruption in racing all over the world, and things were different when everyone came out the other side. After six years of heavy military use, Brooklands was in bad shape and was mostly dismantled; a few remnants of the oval, along with some restored buildings, remain today. Nor did the postwar austerity seem to leave room for the spectacle of mostly well-off young people gallivanting around tracks in expensive cars, least of all women, who especially in Britain were expected to help the country get back on its feet. Of the major races, the Mille Miglia resumed in 1947, the Targa Florio and Monte Carlo returned in 1948, and Le Mans made its comeback after a decade in 1949; Germans were banned from all racing until 1951. The automakers, which had been shut or otherwise occupied with military production, refocused on passenger vehicles, including sports cars, and for the first time foresightful Europeans saw that there might be a market for their type of vehicles in the United States. The action, the fun, and the excitement were about to shift elsewhere.

QUEEN OF THE EAST

It's so hard to go slow.
—EVELYN MULL

When John and Evelyn Mull ran their first novice races at Thompson Speedway on Memorial Day weekend 1953, postwar car racing on the East Coast was shifting from first into second gear. That it was happening at all was largely because of the efforts of a small group of friends who, as young, privileged, car-mad, East Coast Anglophiles back in the 1930s, had been devoted readers of the British specialist magazines and sometimes got to attend races across the Atlantic on summer vacations. Without this connection to Brooklands and English automobiles, American sports car racing would not have come about as it did.

At the center of the group were the three Collier brothers, Barron Jr., Miles, and Sam, of the famous magazine family, who pursued their addiction to elegantly appointed speed through St. Paul's prep school and on to Harvard and Yale. With a few other Ivy League pals, they formed the Automobile Racing Club of America (ARCA) and, on private estates around New England and New York, were able to hold several road races from 1934 until World War II began. Enamored of the racing he witnessed at England's premier speedway, Miles bought a Brooklands Riley and brought it back to one-up his brothers at club conclaves. Crucially, one of Miles's classmates at Yale was a wealthy and enterprising gearhead named Briggs Cunningham, who was to become the dominant figure in East Coast sports car racing in the 1950s. The ARCA staged its final race at the New York World's Fair in 1940—Briggs was keen to run in it, but honored a promise to his mother not to—and was dissolved (temporarily, the founders hoped) two days after Pearl Harbor.

The ARCA, as it turned out, was never reconstituted, but its modest beginnings pointed the way for the postwar resurrection of sports car racing. In 1944, a small group of upper-crust Bostonians convened to create the Sports Car Club of America (SCCA). Elitist to an almost comical degree, these gentlemen were alarmed above all by the wartime practice of trashing old cars for metal and spare parts, and their by-laws mandated the expulsion of a member for selling a sports car without the permission of board members. The SCCA had no thought initially of staging races—in all events, wartime gas rationing effectively prevented it. But after the war, when the ARCA unexpectedly failed to make a comeback, the SCCA, starting with a core roster of seventy-nine members, eventually took it upon itself to revive road racing in the United States.

In July 1947, the SCCA got some engines running at a speed event—the motorized equivalent of a short-distance foot race—at Thompson and a hill climb at Mount Equinox, Vermont. But it wasn't until the following year that the town of Watkins Glen in west-central New York State was convinced to host a genuine road race on a challenging course through 6.6 miles of surrounding rolling countryside. The gathering on October 2 was a spiffy event that provided a showcase for wealthy owners of prewar classics, including Lagondas and Stutzes and Mercedes and Maseratis. In all, some thirty vintage beauties lined up two-by-two in the village center for two separate races, a "Junior Prix" and a "Grand Prix." Among the oddities was something called a BuMerc, which Briggs Cunningham, driving in his first races ever and finishing second in both, concocted out of a Mercedes SSK body (the remnant of a wreck) with a Buick engine dropped into it. Sam and Miles Collier took part, as did former fellow ARCA member Frank Griswold, winner of the final ARCA race in 1940, who picked up where he left off by capturing both the Junior and Grand Prix in a prewar Alfa. A crowd of about ten thousand that bunched up right alongside the roads without a thought to any risk made the day a success, spurring optimism and motivation for more like events.

By the time drivers gathered for the second Watkins Glen races a year later, SCCA membership had jumped to five hundred, and it kept multiplying over the years in leaps and bounds. The organization issued its first racing licenses for women in 1952, and as of 1957, as the zeal for sports car racing was reaching its peak, the club could boast more than ten thousand drivers; of these, about three thousand were licensed for full competition, including sixty-one women. What had started, then, as an exclusive old school club had expanded into an organization open to anyone with a reasonably serious interest in racing.

To compete in SCCA events during the 1950s, potential competitors had to pass muster with the organization's Contest Board. Driving schools were set up at most of the major courses—Watkins Glen, Lime Rock, Thompson, Bridgehampton, Elkhart Lake, Riverside, and others—where aspiring speedsters could learn the techniques of sports car driving from racers themselves. Normally, an expert would give a demonstration for the class, whereupon the instructors, who could number as many as a dozen at a session, would drive with individual students to show how and when to shift and brake to adjust speeds, how to take corners, accelerate out of them, and so on. Evelyn Mull frequently volunteered at Bridgehampton (once she mastered downshifting, that is) and found that one of the trickiest moves to teach was "heel-and-toeing," a technique for conserving motion prior to downshifting. "Instead of braking, stepping on the gas, and braking again, I put my right heel on the brake and right toe on the accelerator to rev up the motor while my left foot is double-clutching. This maneuver does not come naturally to most new drivers."

There had rarely been anything like this in any sport—hands-on tutorials given by front-rank practitioners, and on top of that, they were free; a nominal five dollars was charged for the safety equipment the tracks were required to have on hand. Today, one can spend into the thousands of dollars to attend driving schools run by Bob Bondurant and others who have built the field into a minor industry. In the 1950s, instructors volunteered their time, doing so, in Mull's view, "for the good of the sport." Novices needed to attend three classes that, if passed, enabled them to receive a temporary license good for entry in regional SCCA races. If they coped with these satisfactorily, they became eligible for a license providing access to national events.

In line with their elite sporting origins and the SCCA's explicit identity as a club, races were rigorously amateur. Unlike the situation in Europe, races in the United States were run just for trophies; not only were cash prizes banned, but so were donations from sponsors and car makers and owners and transportation companies. Even incidental freebies like food, drinks, and hotel rooms were out of bounds, although there were always stories of minor under-the-table exchanges. Implicitly, then, the majority of participants were in the game for the excitement of it, for the fun, along with the social aspects. It also meant that you had to bring your own car to race, or have access to one. For this reason, sports car racing transparently favored the wealthy, people like the Mulls who thought nothing of going to Europe every year and bringing back the latest model Jag, or those who could pop around Max Hoffman's Park Avenue showroom and cherry pick from among the recently arrived Alfas, Porsches, and Mercedes.

At the same time, however, the sport didn't have to be all that expensive. As the SCCA's membership rolls expanded, so did the demographic of those involved. The list price of a new entry-level MG remained close to $2500 throughout the 1950s. At the high end of production sports cars was the Jaguar Roadster at roughly $3800 by late in the decade, while the prices of other popular marques—Triumph, Austin-Healey, Alfa Romeo, and Porsche—fell in between. In other words, if you were a gainfully employed middle-class professional and made a car your top priority over any other indulgence, cost did not represent an insurmountable barrier. Especially in California, the ranks of sports car drivers came increasingly from those who worked for a living and drove on weekends out of passion.

All the same, a natural hierarchy prevailed among these nonprofessionals. As the sport hit its stride in the mid-1950s, what all but the wealthiest ambitious drivers wanted was to get a "ride" with one of the select "entrants," one of the handful of wealthy men who bought, engineered, adapted, maintained, and entered cars in races around the country and, to an extent, internationally. These men were the first to bring Ferraris and other advanced race cars into the United States; they had garages and full-time mechanics to work on the vehicles, and, eventually, great vans in which the vaunted cars were transported. To drive for such a team conferred great prestige and a better chance of winning given the quality of the machines. There was no tenure in these relationships, however; you had to do well pretty consistently, as there were many others angling for the few slots with the top entrants.

The paragon among entrants was Briggs Cunningham. A true gentleman and sportsman of the old school, Cunningham had been indoctrinated in British ways at Groton, made numerous European Grand Tours with his mother during the 1920s, and became enamored of race cars after meeting early-days champion Ralph DePalma while at Yale. (His extraordinary collection of seventy-one vintage vehicles eventually occupied its own museum in Costa Mesa, California.) For a long time, Cunningham was known for a witticism he disowned: "The only way to make a small fortune building race cars is to start with a large fortune." Whoever coined it, the joke perfectly expresses the fact that amateurism demanded a great deal of discretionary money of an entrant. Cunningham had it and spent it, although he couldn't pass any along to his drivers, volunteers all. He was a very good, steady racing driver—best, he allowed, in long races such as Le Mans, where he began taking his own cars and drivers in 1950 and where he once drove nineteen and a half hours of it himself. For a number of years Cunningham represented American sports car racing at its classiest, providing in the process a natural target and opponent for upstart Californians as the decade progressed. And oh, yes, he was also a yachtsman par excellence, skippering the *Columbia* to victory over the Brits in the America's Cup Race of 1958.

Although an Easterner in every outward respect—he lived in Connecticut—Briggs Cunningham was originally from Ohio, and the other Eastern entrant of note was also technically a Midwesterner. The surpassingly wealthy Jim Kimberly, heir to the Kimberly-Clark paper and Kleenex fortune in Neenah, Wisconsin, started buying European cars before World War II and began racing in 1950. That year, Kimberly himself helped find the spot for the first Elkhart Lake public roads course and took the feature race in his gorgeous new Ferrari 166 Barchetta, for which he had paid an unheard-of $20,000.

On July 23, 1950, at the same event, what by all accounts appears to have been the first ladies' race run anywhere under SCCA auspices took place. Sally Chapin was the winner of the fifteen-mile contest in Kimberly's Healey Silverstone, followed by Mrs. Corwith Hamill of Wayne, Illinois, in her family's Allard, and Mrs. George Severens of Lake Forest, Illinois, in an MG TC. Inexplicably, no women's races were run in the subsequent two years, even though Elkhart Lake grew enormously, both in terms of entries and attendance, over that time.

As for Kimberly, the tall, silver-haired bon vivant and consort to Hollywood stars, notably Ginger Rogers and

Ann Miller, built up his fleet and enjoyed his biggest year in 1954, when his team took the SCCA C-Modified National Championship with eight wins out of sixteen events, just as Kimberly personally outlapped everyone else on the circuit by a wide margin. Later, as a longtime president of the SCCA, he instituted such long-overdue safety precautions as good helmets, flameproof driving suits, and roll bars.

The number of sports car racing events in the East increased at a gradual pace, mainly because of the lack of suitable venues. With some longtime Long Island locals still able to recall the Vanderbilt Cup races early in the century, and younger enthusiasts remembering Tazio Nuvolari's victory in the Cup's brief revival in 1936, a Bridgehampton road race was scheduled for June 11, 1949, when Briggs Cunningham turned up in the first Ferrari—a Spyder Corsa—to be seen in American competition. This network expanded with new venues at Palm Beach Shores in Florida and in Westhampton, Long Island, in 1950. But it was at Watkins Glen that year that tragedy struck post-war American sports car racing for the first time, when ARCA co-founder Sam Collier was killed in an accident while driving the very same Ferrari Corsa. When a new endurance race was inaugurated at an old air base near Sebring, Florida, on New Year's Eve, the co-founder, Miles Collier, named it after his brother.

Unfortunately, it would take more than this for race organizers to seriously address safety issues on public courses. In just four years, attendance at Watkins Glen multiplied fifteen-fold, to 150,000 in 1951, yet officials provided no barriers between the surging crowds and the speeding vehicles other than knee-high bales of hay on the edges of the roads. Finally, at that year's race, everyone's worst fears were realized: A seven-year-old boy was killed by a passing car, and a dozen more spectators were injured. The race was halted at once, and the future of public road racing looked dire. The final straw came the following spring at Bridgehampton, where, on May 22, Robert Wilder was killed during practice and, the next day, three onlookers were injured when a Jaguar flipped over. The days of racing on public roads were numbered; purpose-built courses would have to be created.

As the racing scene developed in these early years, so—gradually—did the presence of women in it. After Sally Chapin at Elkhart Lake, the next woman in the eastern half of the country to make her presence felt was Suzy Dietrich, who started driving sports cars on hill climbs in her native Ohio with her husband, Chuck, in 1951. Chuck Dietrich was one of the most prominent Midwestern drivers from the dawn of the sports car era, beginning in a supercharged MG TC before moving on to a Lester MG and then becoming the first American to own and race the Elva (a British make so named for its meaning in French—*elle va!* ("she goes")). With Carl Haas, Dietrich later became the U.S. importer of the Elva, which enjoyed a measure of success in production-car racing into the 1960s. Dietrich himself raced for an almost unheard of fifty-two years, until 2002, competing at sixty-three venues.

Chuck taught Suzy the ropes in his MG TC, and she got a boost by finishing first in her class in her initial race, at Chanute Air Force Base in Illinois in 1952; two other Midwestern women, Sally Chapin and Peggy Wyllie, also took part. Suzy drove each successive edition of the Elva but was most associated with the Porsche 550 Spyder: "Man, I fell in love with that car," she exclaims a half century later. Enormously cute with her dark hair cut short in future Jean Seberg style, Suzy was also one of the most aggressive drivers on the track, man or woman. John and Evelyn Mull may have been "The Popular Couple," as they were socially known, but Chuck and Suzy were the fastest husband-and-wife sports car racers in the East; on the West Coast, only Bob Drake and Mary Davis could have given them a run for their money. Suzy, who worked as a librarian in Sandusky, Ohio, for thirty-one years, competed at so many events that, with roughly twenty first-place finishes, she may have captured more victories than any other woman during the

1950s, at least in the East. In addition to regularly mopping up at strictly local events like Akron, where she dominated, Suzy appeared frequently at Watkins Glen (where she won the first Ladies' Race in her RS Spyder) Elkhart Lake, Thompson, Cumberland, and the rest. Subsequently, she moved on to Sebring and the 24 Hours of Daytona. Ironically, one of her frustrations is that she could never compete in the sports car conclave in her virtual backyard, the annual road race that took place from 1952 to 1959 at historical and scenic Put-in-Bay on South Bass Island in Lake Erie, not far from Cleveland. Chuck was a regular winner there in his Elvas, but women were not permitted to compete. When she asked one year to drive the pace car, she couldn't help but drive it nearly fast enough to win the race.

In eastern racing circles during this early period when comfortable wealth was assumed, there was one woman who may have been richer than all the rest of them put together. Elizabeth Haskell was an imposing blond heiress from New Jersey who bought a Crosley-powered Siata from Briggs Cunningham in 1953 and started running well in eastern regional events. Three years later, she took a Maserati to Argentina to race in the Buenos Aires 1000 km and met Alejandro DeTomaso, a dark, brooding twenty-eight-year-old politician's son who had inherited significant money and forsaken political ambitions of his

own in an attempt to follow in the slipstream of his celebrated racing countrymen, Juan Manuel Fangio and
Froilan Gonzalez. An anti-Perónist already keen to leave
Argentina, he quickly did so with Elizabeth, who now
called herself Isabelle, and they were married in March
1957, at Palm Beach.

Although neither became an absolutely top-tier
driver—DeTomaso had early on earned the nickname *El
Insano* for his temper and fierce, fearsome track habits—
they were frequently in the thick of things. As a team, they
had one of their best outings at the January 1958 12 Hours
of Sebring, where, in an O.S.C.A. shared with Bob Fergu-
son, they won first in class and the Index of Performance.
Moving to Modena, Italy, home of Ferrari (Alejandro was
half Italian), they became works drivers for O.S.C.A., and
that June intended to team at Le Mans. However, Isabelle
was informed that France's most famous race was closed
to women, a policy that stemmed from the fatal crash suffered by her friend Annie Bousquet at the 1956 Rheims 12-
Hour race, where Isabelle was her co-driver, as well as
from the disasters of 1955 Le Mans and 1957 Mille Miglia,
where many spectators had been killed.

For their part, John and Evelyn Mull became complete
addicts to racing, she more than he. By turns imperious,
eccentric, blunt, and accomplished, Evelyn had led a
complicated life that only really found a measure of sure

footing when she married the wealthy and piercingly intelligent industrialist in 1946. It was a tangled path that led to the couple's happy equilibrium, a road littered, as it often was among the rich and privileged, with tragedy, instability, and enough melodrama to pack a tumultuous eight-hundred-page multi-generational novel.

John Barnes Mull, born in 1901, was heir to the Barnes and Tucker Company, one of the leading soft-coal mining concerns in Pennsylvania. At its peak, in 1923, it produced more than a million tons of bituminous coal. Never entranced by the family business, John was a spectacular scholar, tearing through St. Mark's boarding school, entering Princeton at sixteen, moving on to Oxford, then returning to Princeton as an instructor of Latin and Greek. He married before turning twenty, to Grace Lansing. When his father abruptly died, John reluctantly but decisively left academia to take charge of the family home of Moshannon Farm at Malvern, just west of Philadelphia. A beautiful 130-acre estate well off the main road, it was thick with woods and had fences built especially for fox hunting. It was also a working farm, with a huge barn for cattle and a stable for horses as well as cottages for the caretaker and the groom (later used by the car mechanic). The colonial-style main house was large but not a mansion. Unusual for the time, it had a pool, down a hill from the house. John, a rangy fellow with thinning hair, exacting standards, and a ferocious temper, also took charge of the family business, which thrived under his stewardship from the 1920s through the World War II years. He divorced Grace, who went on to marry Listerine heir Gerard Lambert. His second wife was a Philadelphia showgirl, Helen Carlin, with whom he had a son, Anthony, and a daughter, Ruth. Then, at a horsy-set social gathering toward the end of the war, he met Evelyn Cary Smith.

Evelyn, born in 1913 in New York, was the oldest child of Courtland Smith and Elinor Cary Smith. Courtland often bankrolled scientists and investors, and as a backer of Pathé News had a hand in the creation of the first sound newsreels and documentaries. Family lore had it that the actress Mabel Dodge had been in love with Seward Kerry, Evelyn's maternal grandfather.

But childhood was not an easy ride for Evelyn. Her parents divorced when she was eleven, and she was dispatched to Foxcroft School in Virginia, where she was conveniently out of the way and became preoccupied with horses. In the coming years, both of her brothers would die, Orlando as a youngster to polio and influenza, and Archie—a star athlete, especially in hockey—from a car accident in Edgartown, Martha's Vineyard. She remained haunted by this, and on her deathbed a half century later, she cried out, "Why was I the only one who survived?"

Exiled from family life, Evelyn was beset by the feeling she had something to prove, especially to her father, who was very tough on her. She felt that the most significant lifelong legacy he left her was teaching her how to drive on Long Island when she was eleven; she had no other pleasant memories of him. Getting away by starting a family of her own, she married George Partridge Mills, a St. Paul's and Yale man from a prominent Minneapolis family. The first of their three daughters was Elinor, called Ellie, born in New York City in 1934, and two years thereafter came Marion, commonly called Nonny. Then, eight years later, early in 1944, Louisiana was born. For what one can only assume were powerful reasons, George never believed that Louisiana, or "Poppy," as she has always been known, was his own daughter. Whatever the truth of it, he and Evelyn divorced four months after Poppy arrived and she and her three daughters ended up in Philadelphia, where two years later Evelyn married John Mull, with John officially adopting Poppy. This upper-class marital drama, replete with whispers of illegitimacy, was so heavily covered in the Philadelphia papers that the family sought temporary retreat in Santa Fe (Mabel Dodge country), where the thoroughbred foxhunting horses they brought out for coyote hunts suffered from altitude sickness.

This happenstance marked the tipping point for John

and Evelyn's primary pastime. When the family returned to Moshannon Farm in 1949, new European cars began supplanting the horses in the stables, to the consternation of neighbors. But the raised eyebrows and complaints about noise were easy to withstand after the brutal gossip that had accompanied John's divorce and remarriage.

Once the Mulls made their headlong dive into racing in Connecticut over the Memorial Day weekend in 1953, they happily arranged the rest of their lives around the sport. With the zealotry of the recently converted, they transformed their four-horse van into a carrier for two cars. Hitting every race within driving distance of Eastern Pennsylvania, and some further afield, they pursued a regular routine in preparation for an event: They packed each of their cars with the necessary racing garb, including fireproof coveralls (always a red garment and helmet for Evelyn), and loaded them into the van, which was driven by their mechanics Walter Huggler Jr. and Chris Wilson (neither John nor Evelyn could as much as change a spark plug); if John was planning to drive in multiple events, a third car could be pulled along behind. They then stocked their station wagon with all the food, drink, coolers, folding chairs, and other paraphenalia normally associated with a day at the beach. Next day, usually a Friday, they drove from Pennsylvania to their destination— which, if it was Lime Rock, Thompson, Bridgehampton, or some other New England course, was generally five or six hours away; whenever possible, they would make it a family affair by bringing along one or more of their daughters. Motels were usually basic and far from luxurious, but the social aspects always more than made up for this shortcoming. Saturday mornings were normally devoted to transporting cars to the track, receiving race numbers for the cars, and lining up for technical inspection, while afternoons were given over to practice runs. Saturday nights could be used for a proper night's sleep, but were much more likely to be devoted to serious socializing and drinking; New England religious propriety wasn't the only reason drivers' meetings weren't called until noon on Sundays. The races themselves were conventionally held between two and six in the afternoon. Sunday evenings—for the Mulls, anyway, as they didn't have jobs to report to the next morning—were the equivalents of gearhead tailgate parties devoted to breaking down every aspect of the races. Driving back on Monday and unloading, the couple would, during peak season, have just three full days at home before packing up and doing it all over again.

This is how the Mulls and quite a few others lived for nearly six months of the year, from May until October, through much of the 1950s. For John, it was something new, a fresh pastime, something he enjoyed and did well, even if he never entered the charmed circle of top-drawer drivers. For Evelyn, it was purer, more elemental; she always professed to love racing. After Thompson '53, she said, "Nothing could keep me off the course." And nothing did. John had a couple of curious reactions to the realization that his wife was better at this new game than he was; he refused to drive against his wife in same class races, and he insisted that she wear skirts at all times except while racing, whereas the norm for women around tracks was shorts or pants. Evelyn was able to put a cheery spin even on something this absurd, noting at the time that, "The problem was solved for me by a friend who made several cotton playsuits consisting of shirt-waist, shorts, and button-down-the-front skirt. So now I am able to unbutton the skirt and step into my coveralls without competing with Gypsy Rose Lee."

Coveralls to the side, there were certain aspects of 1950s racing attire that were sexy in and of themselves—helmets and goggles, leather gloves, sometimes scarves and aviator-style jackets—and some of the women cultivated a particular look for the track. Short hair was common—Denise McCluggage, Suzy Dietrich, Ruth Levy, and Pinkie Windridge were close cropped, while the styles sported by Isabelle Haskell DeTomaso, Audrey King, Jean Spiedel, and Evelyn Mull weren't much longer, probably to accomodate the helmets. Denise never put much thought into looking fashionable (aside from her trademark polka dot helmet and jacket), but others, including hangers-on and "track fluff," as the men called them, amplified the style with trendy Capri pants, ballet flats, colorful shirts, and often wild sunglasses. With its Italian influence, this look, pulled off successfully, was a spectacular complement to the cars themselves, adding a special *je ne sais quoi* allure to a sport already enhanced by the aura of money, speed, worldliness, and risk.

Evelyn's style was conservative by comparison—she was known to wear a necklace to the track, something the women a decade younger would never have dreamed of doing—her manner regal, imperious at times. But her talk was direct, funny, and smart, her outlook upbeat and on the bright side; her children remember her as always going up the stairs singing, "Pack up your troubles in your old kit pack . . . ," feeling that summed her up. She was a big fan favorite because she could give men a tough race and looked good doing it; because of her height and beauty and social status, Evelyn got her picture in the papers far more than did considerably more prominent male drivers.

Even though the racing season in the East was spotty in 1954—Bridgehampton was off the calendar, due to the previous year's spectator injuries, as was Elkhart Lake, with the new Road America under construction—the

Mulls and other Eastern enthusiasts still found events to fill their nearly every weekend. Watkins Glen was back, Thompson and Cumberland were busy, and there were always smaller local venues and hill climbs to sharpen skills. John took a particular liking to rallies and fittingly so for a man whose vast library was festooned with hundreds of watches, all set to Greenwich time.

The following year was a pivotal one for Evelyn as well as for racing. New purpose-built road-racing-style venues were opened, and just in time, due to the groundswell of feeling against the dangerous conditions at public road events. The way spectators spilled over the curbs along smalltown streets, jammed up against the flimsy snow fencing erected as barriers, lounged behind or upon bales of hay scattered along the courses, or just stood around near the pit areas and in more isolated areas of rural roads, it's surprising there weren't far more incidents. Coincidentally, it was in this year, on June 11, that the worst disaster in auto racing history took place at Le Mans when, three hours into the twenty-four-hour marathon, Pierre Levegh's Mercedes hit Lance Macklin's Austin-Healey at more than 130 miles per hour and was catapulted onto an earthen retaining barrier and then to the top of a tunnel, causing a breakup that sent sections of engine, suspension, and wheels flying into the crowd opposite the pits along with other pieces of flaming wreckage, killing more than eighty people. Incredibly, the race continued, although the Mercedes team eventually pulled its cars off the track, and then withdrew from racing altogether.

Evelyn Mull clocked many miles of racing that summer and attracted journalists like the Pied Piper. Typical of the quaintly paternalistic treatment female drivers often received—few write-ups ever failed to note the women's appearance—was the *Road & Track* assessment of her solid drive in the Mount Equinox hill climb, a 5.2-mile course that contained thirty-six sharp curves and ten muscle-testing hairpins, a run that took an everyday car and driver at least fifteen minutes to complete: "Evelyn Mull, the only entrant [out of fifty-one] of the fair sex, sailed her Jaguar to third place in class being clocked at 5 minutes 50.7 seconds. She drew warm signs of approval from the crowd as one of the most relaxed drivers of the day. On the tight double hairpin turn before the finish, she rewarded the male cheering section with the most amiable smile we ever saw."

Increasingly, she wanted to prove herself against all comers; she felt she was very close to being able to equal her male competition. At Watkins Glen, in the final year on its second course layout, Evelyn was running strongly in her Jag until it broke down. In the hundred-mile President's Cup race at the Fairchild Airport course at Hagerstown, Maryland, Sherwood Johnston repeated his Watkins Glen overall win, as well as in Class C Modified, with Evelyn a rather abashed third . . . and last, as all the other cars failed and were forced to retire.

With 1956 came the breakthrough. The season started early, in March, with the 105-mile "Colletonian" at Walterboro Army Air Field, where Evelyn was the only woman entered. In April, John won the rare race—the Class DM event in his Austin-Healey 100F at an average speed of 65.62 miles per hour. In May, at Cumberland for the SCCA's national championship races, there was an unusual assembly of husband-and-wife teams; on hand in addition to John and Evelyn were Chuck and Suzy Dietrich, R. J. and Peggy Wyllie, George and Ann McClure, Mr. and Mrs. Max Steele, and Mr. and Mrs. R. E. Mason.

Then, on June 30 and July 1, Evelyn was the sole woman on the card at Thompson Raceway, where it had all begun for her three years earlier. She scored a hat trick, prevailing in three events. In the initial Saturday one-hour race, she won in Class H modified for under 1500cc cars in a Deutsche-Bonnet, and in an hour-long Class E over 1500cc test, she piloted her black A.C.-Bristol to victory.

The clincher came in Sunday's ten-lap contest for Class E production cars. Cool as a cucumber, she eased the Ace-Bristol around the two miles of asphalt with absolute assurance, handling the hills and twists as if she knew them in her sleep. Denise McCluggage was there to observe it for the *Herald Tribune* and twice exulted at how "smooth" Evelyn's performance was. Not only had Evelyn triumphed in three races over the weekend, but she became the first woman to beat male drivers in any SCCA-sanctioned races. She was the indisputable queen of the East.

There was a bit of a fuss about her afterward, but Evelyn spoke modestly, even self-deprecatingly, insisting that she always got "terrible butterflies" in the moments before a race that all then disappeared the moment she took off, and stressing how she believed "handling a car is more important than speed. I'll never ride or drive anything that's out of control."

East Coast owners and drivers, inheritors of financial and sporting legacies that in some cases could be traced back generations, accepted supremacy at the auto game as something very close to a birthright; for men like Briggs Cunningham and others, they were the natural custodians of the tradition of Anglocentric gentlemen's racing in the United States. But they had already begun

to hear challenging rumbling emanating from points
west, noises that became louder and louder with each
short season. And there was an upstart who was in the
process of burrowing up from their own midst to prove
that neither bloodlines nor money were necessary to be
the best.

THE ICONOCLAST

Racing was something I did, it wasn't who I was. I was a journalist who did this.

—DENISE MCCLUGGAGE

I t looks like it was a career. But it wasn't planned. It couldn't have been planned," maintains Denise Mc-Cluggage, and it is true; no one could ever plan, predict, or count on the sort of extraordinary patchwork quilt of a life that Denise willed for herself. She started as a newspaperwoman more than fifty years ago and remains one to this day, so it is natural to accept that as her professional identity. But she simply could not be content to remain a detached, inactive observer, so she soon started doing what she wrote about—skiing, and then auto racing. She represents the opposite of the old canard about those who can do, do and those who can't do, teach; that which she could write about, she also did. She was a distaff

George Plimpton a decade earlier, but for her it was not a stunt. During the heyday of sports car racing in the mid to late 1950s, she reached a unique sort of career zenith when she drove in races she was ostensibly there to write about for the *New York Herald Tribune*; the clever ways she developed to slip in the news of her own victories under her own byline are a joy to behold. She is a plainspoken Kansan, thoughtful and eloquent; she looks a person or a car or a predicament straight in the face, sizes it up for what it is and speaks the truth about it as she sees it. She has known everyone in the racing world since the 1950s, and she was a friend and/or competitor (and sometimes lover) of many of them: Phil Hill, Stirling Moss, Juan Manuel Fangio, Carroll Shelby, Masten Gregory, Briggs Cunningham, the Rodriguez brothers, Alfonso de Portago, Wolfgang von Trips, Steve McQueen before he was Steve McQueen. As for the women in the field, she as easily teamed up with them as she competed against them. And she has written about her colleagues superbly; a master of the feature-length profile, Denise learned well from newspaper writing how to evoke a personality or an event in deft, definitive strokes. There is much of Hemingway in her ability to tersely describe people and action, and to suggest layers of feeling and meaning through a purposely restrained, often droll style. After her friend the late Ken Purdy, she may be the best writer about racing and racers.

141

The car-racing fraternity was scarcely the first male bastion Denise infiltrated. In 1931, when she was four years old during the Depression in Topeka, Kansas, she asked Santa Claus "for a doll on roller skates and an Austin," and within a few years she was a big tomboy, "the best blocking back on the block" in tackle football, playing in pickup basketball games, riding horses and bikes. At school she played girls' softball, but was never much for organized sports or less rambunctious games like tennis and golf. "There were no boys in the family and I awfully wanted to be one," she says. "I not only played men, I was the leader. Always in demand."

She loved baseball and became a big fan of the Topeka Owls, the local Class C team she could watch for free because a girl in her class was a ticket taker. Along with the blues, she listened to reconstituted big-league games on the radio (not live accounts but summaries related by announcers not present at the games themselves), and occasionally got to the big city to see the Kansas City Blues, a Yankee farm team. Stan Musial came through as a member of the St. Louis farm club, and she saw Bill Rigney, Joe Garagiola. "I was into lonely pursuits."

And from an early age there were cars. When she was about ten, Denise's parents Robert, a lawyer and eventual member of the U.S. District Attorney's office, and mother Velma Faye, a court reporter, took her and her two sisters (another sister had died at five of measles and pneumonia) on a vacation to neighboring Colorado. "My first 'race' car experience was during that time. In Manitou Springs, I remember kiddie-sized race cars on a little dirt track that I think cost a dime a lap. They were probably capable of about ten miles an hour. I remember being thrilled putting my foot down hard. I was one with Louis Unser, my hero." The family also attended the famous Pikes Peak hill climb. Even though her father had no interest in racing per se, he was fascinated by the drivers' dirt-track technique on the mountain's narrow shelf roads. And there they actually got to see Unser and film him with their eight millimeter camera. Denise remembers seeing another famous driver, Rex Mapes, race at the Kansas Free Fair in Topeka when she was a little girl. She also sat in awe of the daredevil stunts that may have inspired some fantasies, although the furthest into extreme sports she ever went was parachuting.

Like many Midwestern kids at the time, she learned to drive young, getting a driver's license at thirteen. She trained on an automatic; her parents both had Oldsmobiles—her dad an 88, which was the first car marketed with hydromatic drive. Three years later, in 1943, she was off to Mills College, a very good girls' school in Oakland, California, where students were not allowed to have cars. On top of that was wartime gas rationing. But one girl,

Kendall, secretly kept a Model A with a rumble seat, and every so often she and Denise would sneak away across the Bay Bridge to San Francisco. This indiscretion notwithstanding, the Mills policy—"Remember who you are and what you represent"—weighed heavily. The girls felt they were in the vanguard, or that they ought to be, and played at being rebels. "The girls took a pledge, not to not get married, but not to have a 'bourgeois marriage.' Well, a year later most of them were married or engaged." As for Denise, "I almost had a boyfriend." But mostly she concentrated on work, and was rewarded with a Phi Beta Kappa key in philosophy.

By the time she graduated, in 1947, Denise had decided she wanted to be a newspaper reporter. The problem was that the paper she wanted to work for, the *San Francisco Chronicle*, didn't hire women, especially women reporters. She went back to Kansas over the summer to learn typing, and by fall her mother agreed she could return to San Francisco. "I had a few jobs before the *Chronicle*, but I kept going back to see Scott Newhall," who was then the editor of *The World*, the Sunday magazine, and in 1952 became executive director of the whole paper. "I went back the next day and the next day and the next day, and he finally said, 'Let's see if we can find something for you.'

"I got a job in advertising. But it was the *Chronicle*. I'd go out late for dinner on Wednesday with the Sunday magazine staff and I'd go back with them to help afterward, but the union guys said I'd have to be paid. I was very pro-union, but I had to deal with them, make them see I wasn't taking anybody's job."

She had her foot in the door, but still didn't have a seat where she wanted one, at a desk with a typewriter. But her talent for sport and compulsion for competition helped change that. "They had a softball team, where we'd play other newspapers, and most of the teams were made up of delivery boys and machinists, beefy guys, not reporters, and there I was as the pitcher of our team. After one of the games, Scott Newhall had a little party at his house and I got to talking to him. It was perfectly pleasant, and on Monday my boss asked me, 'What did you say to Scott?' I said, 'Nothing special. I just sort of anticipated everything he might want to hear,' and he said, 'Well, it must have been good,' and from then on he didn't have to hide me anymore."

In a sign of things to come, Denise spent the first $100 she saved up on her first car, a 1936 Chevy she bought from Al Kay, one of her colleagues on the magazine section. "I couldn't drive it, though, because it had a weird gearshift. The drama critic taught me how to drive it. It didn't take long." Sharing an apartment with two college chums in a Portuguese neighborhood on Eighteenth Street

TODD MCCARTHY

in the Mission, she often worked late, then hit a bar or jazz club—one of her favorites was the Blackhawk in the Fillmore District. But she didn't have to go out to hear live jazz; living on the floor above her new place was up-and-coming pianist Dave Brubeck, along with his wife and baby. Brubeck was part of a trio playing at the Geary Cellar downtown, where during that time you could also hear the likes of Sarah Vaughan, George Shearing, and Ella Fitzgerald. Denise's apartment had two pianos, and sometimes Brubeck, Paul Desmond, and Cal Tjader would practice in her dining room. It was the beginning of a major jazz connection for Denise that would continue throughout her life, an affinity shared by quite a few other race drivers.

In what was literally the smallest manner possible, Denise's experience of competitive racing started on a dirt track in Oakland. "A friend at the *Oakland Tribune* was a midget racing nut. He told me about a school that a midget race car owner and his driver were starting and I thought it would make a good story—and an opportunity to be Louis Unser again. I was the only journalist and the only woman around there. Seems I had a knack for driving midgets on dirt tracks. I started going out with the driver and after the races he would let me drive his car on the track to run it out of fuel, until someone decided it was unsafe.

"Then someone put together a women's race in some sort of modified cars. It was a bit of a mess. Anyway, I was always uncomfortable with 'ladies' races,' which were sometimes even called 'powder-puff derbies,' because they seemed to me rather like mud wrestling, staged as a spectacle for men to chuckle over rather than serious competition. But it was a chance to drive, so I put up with the hair-pull aspects."

Before long, she fell in love, not with the midget car driver but with the MG TC that turned up in the window of British Motor Cars. It was a love requited. As for a little while the only woman in San Francisco with such a car, she attracted considerable attention, sometimes unwanted, as when vaguely unsavory hot rodders tried to follow her home late at night; eluding them gave Denise a legitimate opportunity for fast, creative driving. On another front, the ball field once again played a crucial role in her destiny. One weekend Denise and the otherwise all-male *Chronicle* softball squad took on the *South Pacific* road company team, whose six-foot-five third baseman caught her eye. After she hit a single, she made a point of stealing second and then third, where she started jawing and warning the third bagger's teammates not to let him touch the ball because he threw like a girl. "He wasn't much of an athlete," she admits of her future husband, a Brooklyn boy who hated his given name, Myron

Rubin, and tried on a succession of others before settling on Michael Conrad. "He got the Conrad off my bookshelf," Denise allows. What Denise does not admit is that he had anything to do with her decision to leave San Francisco. "I'd already pretty much planned to move to New York," she insists. In 1951, she sold the MG and moved to New York, determined to "tilt with skyscrapers."

Denise McCluggage knew what she wanted to do when she got to New York City—write for a major newspaper—but despite her experience she knew it would be tougher to storm the citadel in this greatest city, and greatest newspaper city, in the United States. Specifically, she wanted to write for the *New York Herald Tribune*, a real writer's paper, in many ways the most likeable and readable in town; it may have lacked the prestige of the *Times*, but its outstanding reporting provided a comprehensive sense of what was going on without the formality and whiff of self-exaltation. It also had Marguerite Higgins, the most famous female journalist of her era and the ideal role model to any woman determined to do what women weren't supposed to do.

Just six years older than Denise, Higgins was best known for pushing her way to where women had essentially never been before, on the front lines of war reporting. Having grown up in Oakland, where Denise had gone to college, Higgins couldn't get a New York newspaper job after graduating from Berkeley and so signed up for graduate school at Columbia, where she snuck into the *Herald Tribune* as a campus correspondent and was shortly promoted to the city desk. But what she really wanted to do was cover World War II firsthand, and she got her wish, initially in England, then on the Continent from 1944. All of twenty-five, she arrived with a colleague ahead of the troops at Dachau, where SS guards famously surrendered to them.

She covered the Nuremberg trials and the Soviet blockade of Berlin, and was appointed Tokyo bureau chief in 1950, just in time for the Korean War. Tossed out of Korea by an American lieutenant general, she was invited back by General MacArthur and the next year shared a Pulitzer Prize for war reporting. Even at this stage, Hollywood was aching to turn Higgins' life into a movie. In 1955, she was walking alongside Robert Capa in Indochina when the legendary photographer was killed by a land mine, and she shortly thereafter covered the French defeat, gaining indispensable background for her book a decade later warning against American involvement in Vietnam. She was Moscow bureau chief, covered the civil war in the Congo, and reported from Washington until eventually joining *Newsday* and dying, in 1966, of a tropical disease, leishmaniasis, she picked up back in Vietnam.

For women, even women as talented and feisty as Higgins or McCluggage, it was next to impossible in the 1940s and 1950s to walk in the front door of a major city paper and get a reporting job. "Women were not allowed certain, straight paths to things," Denise observed, "you always had to learn meandering back roads." It took Denise some time to find the key, but her period of struggling offered plenty of interest, as New York City is prone to do. Moving into a tiny apartment on Morton Street in Greenwich Village, Denise judged jingle contests and was a publicist for hotels. Then one day in the Village, who should she run into but her old third baseman friend Myron Rubin, or whatever his name was that month (it was soon to be Michael Conrad for good). Now there was the time and inclination to get to know each other, and they became a couple, two young lovers against the world looking for the breaks they knew they deserved. Denise upset Michael by predicting he'd make it as an actor by the time he was fifty (she was right, in that he achieved his greatest fame on *Hill Street Blues* as the desk sergeant Phil Esterhaus), but she was sufficiently taken with his dreams that she enrolled in evening acting courses with Sandy Meisner at the Neighborhood Playhouse. One thing they shared was skiing.

Denise had taken it up in California as a college student, going to Badger Pass, where they used a sled as a ski lift. A German refugee, Michael had learned the sport as a child. Now, they were part of something called the Ski Bird Bus Tour to New England, which was divided into two groups: those who had seen skis before, and those who hadn't. As members of the first group, the couple was able to charge for lessons.

They lived in a fifth-floor walk-up on Cornelia Street, and were married for eleven of the twelve months of 1953. That was it for marriage as far as Denise was concerned. As she put it, "At first I had enjoyed the challenge of playing chameleon and turning myself into whatever color necessary, but soon my energies were depleted beyond rejuvenation." Michael, it seems, had a too rigidly conventional view of male-female roles in marriage and life for Denise, who by nature needed to wear the pants in the family at least part of the time. At the very least, Denise was loyal to the Mills College oath and did not fall into a bourgeois marriage; if anything, it was not nearly bohemian enough for her. Michael married three more times, and was in intermittent friendly contact with his first wife over the years.

Fortunately for Denise, this change in her personal life coincided with the break she had been looking for on the professional front. Just as she had when she wormed and cajoled and persisted her way into the *San Francisco Chronicle,* in 1953 she finally finessed a job at the *Herald Tribune* in the women's feature department, working under fashion editor and social maven Eugenia Sheppard. Not exactly her specialty and the pay was peanuts, but it was the *Herald Trib,* damn it, and she was in the door. She covered things of scant concern to Kansas plains girls—fashion shows, openings, the effect clothes had on men. This went on for about a year and a half, whereupon she got the break she always believed would come. At the time, the best-known woman writer on the paper, other than Higgins, was Caroline Anspach, a "sob sister" whose mission was to churn out heart-wrenching human interest stories that would speak directly to female readers; these, along with gossip and advice columns, were what women were presumed to be capable of writing. In early 1955 Denise wrote a female-slanted piece about skiing that impressed sports editor Bob Cooke, who promptly brought her over to the sports pages to cover the winter sport. It was a beat the former reporter was delighted to give up, as he was old, didn't ski, and hated the cold. For Denise, it was like a full-time vacation, as she got to live in and file from Vermont from late autumn through Easter. Within a season, she was an expert and began quietly forging her own style of participatory journalism. Although as scarce as the proverbial hen's

tooth, women sports reporters were not altogether unheard of. In the 1930s, nine-time U.S. Figure Skating
Champion and 1932 Olympic bronze medal winner
Maribel Vinson became the first female sports reporter
for *The New York Times*, writing even as she continued to
compete. In 1937, she was succeeded at the paper by
Maureen Orcutt, another sportswoman herself, a leading
amateur golfer of the era (and daughter of a *Times* editor,
Benjamin Sinclair Orcutt), who maintained her tournament schedule while covering women's golf and writing
a column, "Women in Sports." For most of her thirty-five
years at the paper—she retired in 1972—she was the only
woman on the roughly fifty-man sports beat.

Having proven herself over the winter, come spring
Denise went to work as an all-purpose sports reporter,
covering everything from girls' junior golf tournaments
and tennis to dog-and-pony shows. Denise first met
Briggs Cunningham, to whom she became very close and
for whom she sometimes drove, while covering a series
of junior regattas on Long Island Sound in 1955. Cooke
quickly saw that Denise merited his complete confidence,
and he had only one piece of advice for her as she
branched out: "I told her to ask any question she wanted
and not to worry about sounding ignorant." Not that this
was likely to happen. Denise was more concerned about
the entrenched attitudes of the male sports reporters; the

Herald Trib had a celebrated staff, led by the already legendary columnist Red Smith, who, along with such other illustrious scribes as Jimmy Cannon and Jim Murray, hated automobile racing, feeling that the public went to races more to witness accidents than to appreciate any human skill.

Despite her gender and eventual sport of choice, Denise came to feel that Smith accepted her as a colleague, which humbled her and endeared him to her. As she wrote in a wonderful *AutoWeek* column entitled "The Non-Sport of Kings," years later, "I remember Red Smith as more a dusty rose than 'red.' The years had paled him and powdered him with a pinkness. He seemed to glow softly, like a night light in a dark hallway. His strength was his gentleness. How dear he was to accept this upstart female in a man's bailiwick. Women sports writers were uncommon then and, in the view of many, unnecessary. Red Smith made me feel acceptably ordinary."

The rest of the sporting world was not as accepting as this old pro, however. Denise was generally made to feel that she was "an oddity for being a woman there, but I was covering sports that weren't usually covered. Most sportswriters didn't know how to deal with women, and there weren't many women athletes. They were ill-disguised men, they were freaks. And when it came to racing cars, it was unbelievable."

When Denise went to cover the Indianapolis 500 for the first time on Memorial Day 1956, she found that, not only were women decidedly unwelcome on the track, they weren't even accorded the same access as male sports reporters, as they were kept out of the pits and press box; to interview the drivers, she was forced to speak to them through the chain-link fences. "They hate me out there," she said, "and I hate them." The same went for the World Series in New York, where she was barred from the Yankee Stadium press box as well as, of course, the locker room, leaving her no option but to generate color coverage by wandering around the stands. Not that she even wanted to hang around the players in the dressing room after the game. "Everyone makes a big deal out of talking to the athletes in the locker room, but I don't think *any* reporters should be allowed in the locker rooms. I think that should be a privileged sanctuary for the athletes themselves. Everyone just gets the same quotes in there as everyone else, and it's mainly a kind of macho thing, since most sports reporters are wannabe athletes anyway."

Early on, Denise shrewdly, and sometimes just luckily, began turning the evident adversity to her advantage, and she relished the cloaked astonishment her little coups elicited in her gruff colleagues. One stemmed from an ostensibly women's angle interview with Mrs. Walter

Alston, wife of the Brooklyn Dodgers manager. In the middle of the women's chatty interview, Walter Alston himself unexpectedly turned up "and started saying all sorts of things in an open way. Afterwards, none of the male reporters believed it, because they could never get Alston to say anything, although they knew it was true because of what he said," recalls Denise.

Another of her favorite stories stemmed from her interview with the landlady of the Harlem boarding-house where New York Giants star Willie Mays stayed. "She was a very erudite, intelligent woman, not at all the black 'mammy' type people expected, and I loved writing all the big words she used, because it surprised everyone," Denise enthuses. "At one point Willie came in, and started quietly packing for a road trip. He didn't say much—he was very shy—but he was always present in the background, which added so much to the piece."

And then there were the cars. "It was my choice to cover racing," Denise admits. "They only covered Indianapolis at the time. I kind of wrote my own ticket." Bob Cooke let Denise cover all the races she wanted and gave her all the space she needed. The motivation was purely selfish on the reporter's part, of course. But because of Denise McCluggage's personal enthusiasm, the *New York Herald Tribune* carried the most comprehensive coverage of American sports car racing during the golden years of the mid to late 1950s of any daily newspaper. Once she started on the circuit in 1955 and 1956, Denise covered as much of the season as humanly possible, traveling from Sebring and Watkins Glen to Bridgehampton, Lime Rock, and Monterey, and covering the opening of Elkhart Lake and the annual Bahamas Speed Week, among many other events. Her dispatches showed up in other papers, including the *Times*, prompting them to beef up their coverage of the sports car racing scene. With this breakthrough, she found she had sculpted a perfect private life from the shape and seasonality of her professional one: Winters skiing in Vermont, summers at racetracks all around the country, in each case writing about it and doing it too. It was as if Hemingway had been a matador in addition to writing about bullfighting. "It was premeditated," she admits. "By covering racing, I could race."

Not long before, she had finally found a replacement for her first MG, the one she had sold before leaving San Francisco. "A fun CBS guy, Art Peck, was a member of the Long Island Sports Car Association, and a florist friend of his, who was also a member, sold me my next MG, an MG TC," Denise recalls. "It was about one year newer than my old one, red, with steering wheel on the right."

One of the first results of her latest automotive acquisition was a special relationship with a young man who was about to become especially famous. For some time, the sight of two cool and rare MG TCs parked near each other, sometimes with bumpers nearly touching, was the subject of much speculation among neighborhood regulars on Cornelia Street, speculation, that is, about when the young and hip owners of the two cars were going to meet and get together.

It finally happened one day in front of Joe's Luncheonette, an all-day breakfast hangout on West Fourth Street, where Denise often stopped for a toasted bran muffin. As she put it in her lovely personal memoir in *AutoWeek*, "He was leaning against his cream-colored MG TC holding a new leather-covered racing helmet and telling someone how some friends in England had sent it to him. And man, that was just too much! Shaking his head." The boyish blond fellow doing the talking, she soon learned, was Steve McQueen, a struggling young actor with a passion for motorcycles and cars. He had paid $750 for the car but at this point had little cash and few prospects, having recently been fired from the touring company of *The Member of the Wedding* in Chicago for his unprofessional behavior and having landed on an unofficial theatrical blacklist as a result; he had yet to make a film. Like Denise, he had studied at the Neighborhood

Playhouse, and this and their shared passion for anything fast gave them plenty in common.

As Denise puts it, "We became a sort of Village *item*,
which surprised me." She liked best the "incongruity"
between McQueen's cockiness and vulnerability, his
brash self-assurance and his little-boy tendency to feel
hurt. She describes their relationship as "no really big
deal," but they reveled in the things that made the
West Village the best place to be if you were young and
with it in those days—the jazz, the Method-acting
scene, the feeling of impoverished superiority to the
Uptown world, and, special to them, the freedom and
apartness fast wheels conferred. Soon McCluggage and
McQueen moved on, she to fuller immersion in the racing scene, he to Broadway (he briefly replaced Ben
Gazzara in *A Hatful of Rain*), Hollywood (he appeared
in his first film, *Somebody Up There Likes Me*, in 1956),
and marriage to Neile Adams the same year. But they
remained fond of each other, catching up periodically in
places like Sebring and Los Angeles and London and
discussing an idea Denise had for a car racing movie
which, in the end, he bypassed in favor of his docu-
mentary-like *Le Mans*.

In the meantime, there were races, more and more of
them. Free to cover whatever meets she felt merited it,

Denise followed her desultory and rain-soaked stay in Indianapolis at the end of May 1956, with a visit to her winter stomping ground to report on the sixth annual SCCA hill climb to the 3800-foot summit of Mount Equinox just outside Manchester in southern Vermont. Hill climbs were popular events with many club drivers, who could use the same cars they drove in sports car races and rallies. As they involved solo runs rather than car-to-car competition, they weren't normally as risky as races. This one, however, was calamitous. Denise witnessed a devastating crash when thirty-one-year-old Paul Flickinger, a nuclear power engineer from Groton, Connecticut, who had won the unrestricted class with his initial run of 5.02.3 minutes in his massive 4 CL Maserati, took out a guardrail about a third of the way up the road in his attempt to break five minutes on his second and final run. The car, which was fueled with alcohol, burst into flames and the driver was pulled out by two spectators. Flickinger was burned over his entire body, however, and died four hours later, leaving his wife and seven-year-old daughter. Although fatalities were uncommon, they were not unheard of at sports car events.

After squeezing in a midweek report from the Women's Metropolitan Golf Association championship in Purchase, New York, Denise hightailed it to Elkhart

Lake, Wisconsin, where the Road America facility had opened to great acclaim the previous September. One of the numerous East vs. West showdowns that were now dotting the racing calendar, this one was won by Jack McAfee from Los Angeles in a John Edgar Porsche Spyder, the same car Jack had driven to victory at Cumberland the month before. Then it was off to Connecticut's Thompson Speedway, which provided the occasion for Denise to observe Evelyn Mull for the first time, and at her best; it was the weekend Evelyn won her three races against male competition. On July 1, Denise filed a report testifying that, "All the races were good ones, one of the best being Evelyn Mull's smooth victory in her smooth, black A.C.-Bristol," a reference to her victory in the race for Class E production cars.

After covering one more golf tournament, Denise set her sights on her goal for the summer: competing as a race car driver. In preparation for this long-planned transformation, Denise bought a brand-new Jaguar XK140MC, a red convertible model and a heavy car. With a confidence based on her success at midget racing and everything she had learned over the years, Denise believed she'd be all right on the track and strategically picked for her debut what she thought would be a modest-size local event: A program of races at an improvised cone-marked airport course at Montgomery, New York, a small town about ninety minutes north of Manhattan and west of the Hudson.

The weekend of August 18–19 turned out to be anything but modest, and so did Denise's entrance onto the racing stage. As she wrote in her wrap story for the *Herald Tribune*, "What started out to be a mere regional race with sports car buffs of the New York region trying their skill on a road-race course laid out on an auxiliary airfield here has taken on all the signs of a national event with entries from all points of the Sports Car Club of America."

In front of some twelve thousand fans, Carroll Shelby, the rangy Texan by way of Los Angeles and the season's premier driver thus far, dominated the weekend in John Edgar's 3.5 Ferrari. Phil Hill, just returned from his triumph at the Swedish Grand Prix, shared a Ferrari with leading French driver Maurice Trintignant, and the crowd got another bonus in that 5 of the 130 cars competing were Porsche Spyders, the greatest number of the new rear-engine speedsters yet seen in one place in the United States.

Denise drove in two of the slate's nine races. In race five, a twenty-five-lap affair for Class C production cars, she finished eighth. The winner was Harry Carter, with an average speed of 63.1 miles per hour, and taking sixth was one of the region's best-known amateurs, show business restaurateur Vincent Sardi; both men drove

XK140MCs. In race eight, the five-lap Women's Race, Denise, in her own Jag, took first place with a 60.5-mile-per-hour time, followed by the little-known Peggy MacKenzie in a Jag XK120, Anise Ash in an MG-A, and Barbara James in a TR-3. In covering the event, Denise avoided writing about her successes; instead, she just matter-of-factly included her name in the lists of race finishers.

Thus did Denise McCluggage, at thirty, take the stage as a driver to whom attention must be paid.

WAY OUT WEST

I know of no field where women get a better break.

—JOSIE VON NEUMANN

When the first-ever racing event was put on at Torrey Pines, a breathtakingly situated and sometimes treacherous circuit on the former Camp Callan army base on a wind-blown bluff overlooking the Pacific Ocean between Del Mar and La Jolla, part of the program on December 9, 1951, was a ladies' handicap. This was something new to the West Coast; never before had there been the drivers to justify one. But that day at Torrey Pines there were several, among them Helen Livingston, in her MG TC; Meyera Zeiler, behind the wheel of a Jaguar XK120, and nineteen-year-old Josie von Neumann, piloting an MG TD, a red number with painted wire wheels specially lightened and lowered for her by her stepfather.

Josie started at the back of the pack and was waved off the line by starter Ralph DePalma a full minute after the first to go, a substantial disadvantage given that the race was only fifteen miles long. But Josie, whose first race this was, went all out from the get-go, flooring it on the straights and smoothly braking and downshifting into third gear on the turns. Whereas the other women seemed tentative, "as if they were stuck in first gear," in the view of eyewitness Bob Dearborn, Josie drove with astonishing assurance for a novice, overtaking her rivals and leaving them far behind by the end. It was a taste of things to come for the talented young kid who won more races in California during the 1950s than any other woman. Many years and dozens of races later, she would become the first female licensed to race by the United States Auto Club.

But Josie was a paradox, a conundrum, and a mystery all rolled into one. Her father was Joe Bigelow, a big radio and, later, television producer for NBC. But her mother Eleanor divorced Joe and subsequently wed John von Neumann, who adopted Josie and became one of the founders and central figures of Southern California sports racing. As John's stepdaughter, Josie was the ultimate insider; she always had the best cars, mechanics, and advice, and never had to go begging for a ride. But she was a squat, homely woman with coarse black hair—"She was built like a box," snipes her frequent rival, the statuesque Mary Davis—and was socially retiring and never joined in the camaraderie enjoyed by the women drivers who came along just after her (and more often than not finished races behind her). The few who engaged her in conversation found her quite personable one-on-one, even sweet, and in her few interviews she comes across as smart and charmingly candid. But increasingly over the years, she seemed to prefer the company of animals and cars to people, an inclination suggested by her enormous menagerie of animals and the nine-vehicle collection she kept at her home in North Hollywood along with an impressive library; she herself was often compared to a solitary cat. "She never came to parties, she didn't get involved with anybody," says race crowd social arbiter Bill Gardner. "She just showed up at the track and raced." To this day, her old contemporaries debate about whether she was really as good as her victory-laden record would indicate, or was largely the beneficiary of top equipment and frequently weak competition.

Whatever else might be said, there is no question that, throughout her career, Josie fought a quiet, steady, and forceful campaign to put women on the same level with men in racing, by action more often than by words. Even from the time of her first race, Josie didn't see why women and men should not compete in races together. "After all, driving isn't a matter of brawn," she maintained, echoing the sentiments of other women drivers through the years. "What counts in today's fast handling cars is brains and stamina. It's been proved that women often have more stamina than men. And in the brain department . . . well, I know a couple of male drivers who aren't exactly Einsteins." To the charge that women are generally more cautious and aren't so inclined to go for broke as are men, Josie agreed that women's big stumbling block is their self-preservation instinct. "But once you've conquered in the pursuits usually denied women, the fear that once held you back becomes secondary."

But no matter how impressively Josie handled her competition and her cars—to prove a point, she stepped up to one of the heaviest, toughest cars to control, a big V-8 Lincoln-Allard, at the Madera Road Races in November 1952 and beat most of the men—she had to content herself more often than not with ladies' races, which in those early years were often unscintillating affairs regarded by large portions of the racing crowd as an excuse to head out for a hot dog or bathroom break. If Josie was running to form, there was seldom much suspense as to who would win.

Josie's stepfather, John, was one of the most compelling figures in American sports car racing, and as Josie was privileged in her time, so had John been as a young man growing up in Vienna during the 1920s and early 1930s. John's eminent surgeon father, Heinrich von Neumann, had extensive Anglo connections, dating to King Edward VIII having been a patient, that made it possible for him to move his family, first to Canada and then to New York City as war approached. In 1939, shortly after they became settled on Park Avenue, Heinrich abruptly died; while his wife and two daughters remained there, his German-accented son joined the U.S. Army. As Michael T. Lynch, William Edgar, and Ron Parravano point out in their indispensable *American Sports Car Racing in the 1950s*, one of John's stops during his military training was the very Camp Callan where he would return a decade later to run cars at Torrey Pines.

In Europe, John had two wartime automotive experiences he was later able to use to his advantage. As the Germans retreated, they left behind countless vehicles, including many high-end Mercedes staff cars that John commandeered for a while before turning them in, provoking not a few stares. Later, assigned to his native Austria to work in the de-Nazification process, John drove an assortment of Volkswagens, developing an affinity for and confidence in the marque that would lead him, just a few years later, to become the pioneer importer of the VW in California; with the Porsche, this would form the basis of his business success with Competition Motors.

Heading to Los Angeles after the war to enroll in the University of Southern California, John jumped right into the intense local car scene. At the time, hot-rodders ruled the roost, but the number of sports car freaks who read foreign magazines was growing. There were a few spots, including drive-in movies and restaurants, where speedsters would congregate and compare cars, and precious few others where they could illicitly run fast—up San Fernando Boulevard toward the Los Angeles Reservoir and Hansen Dam in the San Fernando Valley, along Mulholland Drive, out on Topanga or up remote mountain roads to the north. But there was nowhere to truly race, a situation finally addressed in 1947 by three young men who met at these rendezvous: Roger Barlow, a former documentary filmmaker who, in 1946 in Beverly Hills, opened the first postwar foreign car dealership in the country; his employee Taylor Lucas, and John von Neumann, who soon became a salesman at Barlow's International Motors. The three took it upon themselves to found the California Sports Car Club, with the express purpose of staging races for enthusiasts. The club's first competitive event was a one-lap speed contest—won by John in his 3.5-liter Jaguar SS100—at Palos Verdes on August 31, 1947, thirteen months before Watkins Glen's renewal in the East. Modest though this was, it was a start, and the Cal Club not only came to rival the Sports Car Club of America within California (the two organizations went through bitter periods when their respective leaders were not on speaking terms), but to attract national attention due to the quality of its drivers and success of its events.

As if with the hand brake still on, Southern California racing lurched along for the next couple of years, although its base of young enthusiasts was growing fast, a testament to the relative affordability of suddenly available cars like the MG TC and the wide-open, all-are-welcome attitudes of those involved. This posture stood in marked contrast to the more elitist atmosphere that prevailed in Northern California, where the strong San Francisco Region affiliation with the SCCA kept nascent CSCC influence to a minimum. A couple of abortive and minor events were planned in 1948, and the following year a rival, short-lived club, the Foreign Car Racing Association, staged two events at the dirt track Carrell Speedway in Gardena in July and August. Emerging as a force here by virtue of his six race victories was the twenty-two-year-old Phil Hill, driving his first sports car, a supercharged MG TC acquired from his boss, Barlow. In 1961, Hill would become the first (and, to date, only) American-born world champion Formula 1 driver.

The gentlemen up north stole the upstarts' thunder, however, on November 20, by putting on the first legitimate road race on the West Coast. The course was laid out at Buchanan Field in Concord, thirty miles from San Francisco. Given that the event was largely generated by the local MG Car Club, it was far from surprising that the field consisted of nothing but MGs and was won by Bjarne Qvale, whose brother Kjell would open his British Motor Cars dealership in the city the following year.

In 1950, the Southern California Car Club was at last able to find suitable places to run real road races and organize events more significant than speed contests and hill climbs. Like so many of the "tracks" of the early 1950s, beginning with Buchanan and Goleta, near Santa Barbara—where some time trials had been run the previous August—Palm Springs made use of an airport, in this case an Army Air Corps facility built in the early 1940s as an inland fall-back in case Southern California was invaded by the Japanese; it occupied the same location as the contemporary commercial airport. With the Cal Club having received the blessing of the mayor, silent film star Charles Farrell, the first course was laid out just west of the abandoned air field on a combination of old base roads and unfinished housing development streets. The Cal Club was forced to pay to pave the connecting stretches, and the variable road surfaces made for some interesting driving. The course was altered in stages to include service roads and, ultimately, the runway and tarmac areas came into play, with little bales of hay piled along the sides for demarcation and a small measure of safety. Bill Pollack, a young driver who began his own career placing second in his own MG TC at Santa Barbara and, at the initial Palm Springs gathering on April 16, 1950, finishing first in the novice race and third in the main, recalled, "What was a kick, from a driver's point of view, was the transition from a concrete runway to an asphalt taxi strip. The concrete used for runways is especially rough textured, so your traction was great. The black top was inevitably covered with slippery marbles, and no matter how many times we swept the asphalt turns, there were always a fresh supply of these black ball bearings to give you a thrill." No ladies race took place in Palm Springs that first year, but this didn't stop the irrepressible Irishwoman Fay Taylour from showing up in her MG TD to run head-to-head with the men.

Convening on that blistering Sunday in the desert along with John von Neumann were John Edgar and Tony Parravano. As entrants, these three men soon came to dominate the 1950s California scene thanks to the extraordinary stables of cars they assembled between them and the drivers they attracted around them. While competing with one another, together they would present an imposing West Coast challenge to the supremacy of Briggs Cunningham in the world of American sports car racing.

Naturally, they were all men of means, John Edgar much more so than the others. Von Neumann may not have started with much, but everything he touched he managed to turn to his profit, and his Viennese background gave him a comparatively aristocratic bearing that set him well apart from the likes of a *contadino* such as Tony Parravano. Tony was a real-estate speculator at just the right time in Southern California, a low-bid specialist who got city contracts to build sewers and developed cheap tract housing throughout Manhattan Beach, Gardena, and Torrance. Born in 1917 on a farm south of Rome, in 1934 he moved with his family to Detroit, where his first job was as an upholsterer at Ford. Within a few years, he became the biggest concrete contractor in the Motor City, then headed to Southern California with his wife, Valia, and two sons during World War II. Construction boomed, and he almost inadvertently got into racing after he met mechanic and driver Jack McAfee at the latter's Hermosa Beach mechanics shop in 1948. Tony brought Jack two Cadillacs to soup up and, at the April 1950 Palm Springs event, Tony and Jack made their debut in racing on a winning note when Jack's 1949 Caddy Sedanette beat John Edgar's supercharged 1950 Ford.

Short, thick, and crew-cut, Tony had no formal education and a-talked-a-like-a-dis, with a bit of a left-over rural Italian accent. He threw himself into racing with a passion, but was an erratic character; he endlessly fiddled with cars' engines, to the great annoyance of his drivers and mechanics, was distracted by other business interests and left home for months at a time to buy up cars in Italy or pursue questionable real-estate ventures in Mexico. As John Edgar's son Will observed, "Tony was a fun guy, but impulsive. Idiosyncratic, opinionated. He didn't fit in as well as John von Neumann or my father did. He was kind of an outsider." In 1952, he acquired his first Ferrari, which became the first of its marque to race in California, and by 1955 "Scuderia Parravano" could boast the best and most beautiful car collection of any entrant in the state: five Ferraris, two Maseratis, a Mercedes 300SL and an Alfa Romeo Sprint Coupe. Bill Gardner was with him one night in the Los Angeles freight yards when a special shipment of twenty-five Parravano Ferraris and Maseratis was unloaded from double-deck rail cars for eventual sale. These resources helped him attract many top drivers, including Ken Miles, Jimmy Bryan, Masten Gregory, Bob Drake, Phil Hill, and especially Carroll Shelby, who helped Tony dominate the scene in 1955 and 1956. It also meant that Tony had far more money—the cars alone were valued at about $500,000—tied up in racing than anyone else on the amateur circuit, which is part of the reason that Tony led the charge to push sports car racing in a professional direction.

There were always suspicions, inspired by his origins and Detroit connections and bolstered by untoward events of the late 1950s, that there was something shady about at least some of Tony Parravano's dealings. Bill Pollack, who drove for Tony briefly at the beginning, believed that, "He was a bandit. He'd go to Italy and lend money at usurious rates and two weeks later he'd call the loan. He didn't make many friends doing that. He'd buy cars that all looked like they'd been raced hard and put away wet."

His fate only furthered the speculation about underworld ties. In 1956, he was hit up by the Internal Revenue Service for tax evasion and was later caught trying to smuggle cars out of the United States to Mexico. He quit racing in 1957 and spent much of the next couple of years out of the country, but finally returned, purportedly to square his account. But on April 8, 1960, after picking up some suits from his tailor, he didn't turn up for an appointment in Hollywood. He was never seen again. All manner of unsavory theories filled the local papers. Many years later, remains found buried in Griffith Park were supposedly identified as Tony's via dental records, but the case has never been solved. Tony was forty-three.

Like his contemporary Briggs Cunningham, John Edgar was born—in 1902—to money but otherwise couldn't have been more different. Sports car racing's most outrageous character, John Edgar took his cars and drivers for a wild ride, ensuring he had a grand time all the way and always providing one for his cohorts in the bargain. "He was a dedicated alcoholic," Bill Pollack advised. Bruce Kessler, who drove for him from time to time, said, "You could write a novel about him. John Edgar had a doctor with him at all times. It was a joke how much he drank." But somehow he functioned, he made it all work for him; to paraphrase Stephen Sondheim, he lived it up and died in bed.

Prematurely bald as a billiard ball and thin as a cue stick—"Gaunt doesn't begin to describe him," Pollack observed, while Ruth Levy accurately named writer Hunter S. Thompson as a near look-alike—John spent his twenties and thirties alternating between strained obedience to his strict industrialist father, who ran the Hobart Manufacturing Company in Troy, Ohio, and living a prolonged wild youth. Married at twenty-four to local glamour puss Gigi Getz, John ran booze during Prohibition, drove fast cars and motorcycles and even faster hydroplanes, and was seriously injured in all three. Except for one abortive move to Los Angeles in the mid-1930s with his wife and two boys, John remained loyally in Ohio and anesthetized himself with liquor until 1943, when, with his father's death, a substantial inheritance liberated him from the family business. Back in California, he tried professional photography, ordered a specially built Vincent Black Lightning motorcycle from England that broke the world's speed record, and lodged with his family for four years at the Garden of Allah on Sunset Boulevard, where the likes of Bogart and Bacall, Ronald Reagan, and Errol Flynn provided congenial drinking companions.

As so many others would do in the coming years, John officially started his sports car career when he became one of the first Californians to jump on the MG TC bandwagon, in 1947. Once he supercharged the 1250cc engine, giving it three times the horsepower of a factory MG, the low-slung red buggy became the terror of the Hollywood Hills, where he often ran it with abandon, and in races. John himself drove a few times—in the TC as well as in a supercharged 1950 Ford—through 1951, notably at events in Palm Springs and El Segundo. But the first driver to give entrant John Edgar a victory was Pollack, in the TC on October 15, 1950 at the inaugural "Foreign Car Races" at Carrell Speedway, a halfmile, slightly banked dirt oval in Gardena normally used for midget racing, a win that enhanced the little car's reputation as "the giant killer."

John soon began acquiring more cars and drivers. By the mid-1950s, his most notable pilot was Carroll Shelby, who won lots of races in John's cars and, with his beautiful future wife, actress Jan Harrison, joined John and his wife, Gigi, for a lot of memorable nonsense. John, who once waved Bill Pollack into the pit during a practice so he could retrieve a bottle of Scotch hidden inside the door, was on another occasion set up by Carroll and Jan when he called their hotel room to see if they had any liquor. As Bruce Kessler, who was also there, recalled it, "They said yes, come on over and get it. As a gag, Jan lay in the center of the room with a tie around her neck as if dead. John came in, looked everywhere for the booze and never even noticed Jan, or acknowledged her body on the floor."

On a different evening of hotel antics, Bruce was obliged, due to a shortage of rooms, to bunk with John the night before a race. At a certain point, John said he was calling for a couple of hookers and locked Bruce out of the room. "Walter Cronkite and another guy invited me to stay in their room for a while," Kessler recalled. "Eventually, I got back into John's room. I thought he was done. But then in the dark I saw John humping away and saying, 'What nice titties you have,' and eventually I could see there was no one in the bed under him." As far as John's son Will was concerned, it went without saying: "Everybody had a good time driving for my father."

Although the early days of West Coast sports car racing formed a patchwork, almost improvised affair, the sport was a wild, endlessly colorful party due to the fantastic assortment of venues as well as cars and drivers. On June 25, 1950 there was a race at the Santa Ana Blimp Base. On November 5, six weeks after Sam Collier had been killed driving at Watkins Glen, a new course debuted in California that was both stunningly beautiful and exceedingly treacherous—Pebble Beach, along the coast at Carmel. During its seven years of existence, Pebble Beach represented the benchmark event for sports car road racing west of the Mississippi. The glorious 1.8-mile course on the private Del Monte Properties, where the prestigious golf tournaments were held, consisted of narrow roads that wound through pine forests that were frequently shrouded in fog. It was, in the opinion of Bill Pollack—who won there twice—"a scary place to drive because there was no place you could make a mistake and live to tell about it. The whole course is surrounded by trees, and there are people all around."

Pebble Beach's origins offer further proof of how many of the roads used in American auto racing figuratively started in New Haven, Connecticut. In league with driver Sterling Edwards, Pebble Beach was the brainchild of developer Jack Morse, who had gone to Yale with the Collier brothers, just as his father Samuel had attended the university with future Indianapolis Motor Speedway owner Tony Hulman. That first year, the wealth was spread around, with John von Neumann, Edwards, and Michael Graham all winning preliminary races. But the main was taken by Phil Hill in a Jaguar XK120 with a busted clutch and shot brakes. The tense, enigmatic young man from Santa Monica had been turning up at nearly every race in Southern California from the beginning, but after this win he was now on the map as a driver from whom great things were expected.

Phil Hill, noted for his tremendous concentration behind the wheel, was often called sensitive, cerebral, and withdrawn, at least by race-world standards. He was a rare bird, a mechanical wizard devoted to classical music, and so nervous before races that he would often throw up. Stirling Moss, who knew him well and raced against him often, came to consider him the best sports car driver in the world, although he noted that, "Phil is emotionally so taut, so overwrought much of the time that one would think he'd be exhausted from sheer tension. . . . It's terrible, the tension that builds up in Phil just before a race, though. You can look over at his car and say: 'My God, Phil, the thing's burning!' and he'll jump nine feet into the air. But when the flag drops he's all right." In the 1960s, after he had won his Formula 1 world championship, Phil had a small speaking role in (and drove the camera car for) John Frankenheimer's Cinerama racing movie *Grand Prix*. But Bill Pollack thinks there should have been a Phil Hill *character* in the film, one he feels could only have been played by the neurotically intense actor Montgomery Clift. Denise McCluggage, a girlfriend for a while and a lifelong friend, muses, "Phil kept thinking he shouldn't be where he was. He thought racing wasn't really a proper profession. But that's what he was good at."

As for Bill Pollack, he was the son of Tin Pan Alley and prolific film songwriter Lew Pollack and vaudeville dancer Helen Mellette. He became an army air force bomber pilot who spent most of World War II in Texas. Back in Los Angeles, married, and starting an advertising career in auto magazines with Petersen Publications, he caught the MG bug and began racing his own TC in Santa Barbara in 1949. After a good showing at the initial Palm Springs meet, he was taken on by John Edgar, for whom he drove for a while. Aside from his softspoken wise-guy wit, however, which could have served him well in a second career as a Hollywood toastmaster (a role he has long filled instead at automotive functions), Bill was known for his ability to handle the Allard-Cadillac, a heavy, hard-to-drive car that went like blazes, especially with Bill hitting the gas.

Strictly speaking, the Allard-Cadillac was a hot rod, in that it represented a special combination of elements of different cars. The Allard was a British trial car, designed to be run in demanding conditions against the likes of Austins and MGs, and the racing version, the J2, was simply a rugged chassis into which the buyer could drop any engine he wanted. Owner Tom Carstens, based in Tacoma, Washington, was determined to use a Caddy engine, one of the Detroit powerhouses at the time and a weighty thing to place in the smallish British frame. Further hybridizing the vehicle was a Ford transmission with Lincoln Zephyr gears.

The way Bill came to pilot the car at the second Pebble Beach in May 1951 serves as an excellent illustraton of how loose things were in the early days of American sports car racing. In Hollywood, Bill had once taken a 'round-the-block test drive in an Allard, and was later told by Allard dealer Alan Moss about a guy up in Washington State who was looking for an experienced driver who could handle the car in a race. Bill promptly called Carstens and mentioned his recent victories in his MG TC. "I also told him that I had had a ride in an Allard. I did not specify which seat." With that, Carstens told Bill to meet him at the Standard station garage in Carmel the day before the race.

When Bill arrived for the big event and ignited the

car's engine for first time, he felt that, "The roar and sheer brute power that filled the building was mindful of my flying days and the R-2800 Pratt and Whitney that power the Martin B-26. The car shook, the garage shook, Carmel shook and I shook." He had time for just one late-afternoon spin down Route 1 past Big Sur to get used to this little monster, which was instantly recognizable for its black body, red wire-spoked wheels and white side-wall tires. In practice the next morning Bill won the pole position, and in the main race he was able to out-accelerate everyone at will, including a dogged Phil Hill in a supercharged 2.9-liter Alfa. Two stars were born, an American car that could beat the hot Europeans at their own game, and Bill Pollack, and they repeated the trick the following year.

Another top Southern California driver was Jack McAfee, a Los Angeles kid who served in the Navy and, unusually, had done a lot of sprint car driving before turning to sports models. His expertise was noticed by Tony Parravano, who hired him to work full-time in 1948 and put him behind the wheel during the Palm Springs inaugural races in 1950. Jack (no relation to another prominent mechanic and driver, Ernie McAfee) drove Tony's Cadillac in the first Carrera Panamericana, a grueling five-day marathon on the Pan-American Highway between the Texas border and Guatemala. He drove successfully for Tony and the two Johns in the years thereafter, although it was in the fifth and final Carrera Panamericana, in 1954, that John Edgar's Le Mans-winning Ferrari 375 Plus crashed, injuring Jack and killing his co-driver, Ford Robinson. Jack dropped out for a while, but bounced back in 1956 with wins at Pebble Beach, Cumberland, Elkhart Lake, and Seattle.

One other significant driver was Ken Miles, a tough, hawk-faced Brit who had driven tanks during World War II and, according to Bill Pollack, drove cars the same way, as if he weren't afraid to crash through a wall. At first, Ken was Mr. MG, an almost unbeatable competitor in his self-styled Miles Special and "Flying Shingle" and the dominant driver in the under-1500cc class; in 1953 he notched fourteen straight victories in his Special. When MGs could no longer cut it against the new Porsches, Ken switched, driving Spyders for John von Neumann and then Otto Zipper, and finally Carroll Shelby. He kept moving up against international competition, in 1966 winning the Daytona twenty-four-hour and Sebring twelve-hour endurance races. By rights he should also have won Le Mans that year, as he crossed the finish line first. In one of racing's most freakish disappointments, however, Ken, who was well out in front after having driven an outstanding race, was ordered to slow down by his entrant Ford to allow its two other cars to bunch up

Josie von Neumann in her father's #11 Ferrari.
(Lester Nehamkin photo courtesy of Steve Earle)

Evelyn and John Mull unloading their van.
(Mull Family Archives)

Suzy Dietrich in her
Porsche Spyder.
(Mull Family Archives)

Isabelle and Alejandro
de Tomaso.
(Mull Family Archives)

Denise McCluggage strapping on her signature polka dot helmet, Nassau, 1957.

(Bahamas News Agency)

Evelyn Mull pulls ahead of a D Jaguar in her A.C. Bristol, #72, at Sebring, 1957.

(Mull Family Archives)

Ruth Levy always thought she had an advantage having learned to race her Porsche Speedster on Minnesota's snow and ice.
(Ruth Levy Collection)

New York Herald Tribune reporter Denise McCluggage rounds the haystacks in a Jaguar XK 140M in her racing debut at Montgomery Field, New York, 1956. Afterwards, she said, "I get 15 cents a mile from the paper and I drove 15 miles, so I'm a pro now."
(Photo: Tom Burnside)

Mary Davis in a TR 3.
(Mary Davis Collection)

Carol Givens, "High School" Harry Givens and Ruth Levy
in the cockpit, surrounded by some of the gang.
(Ruth Levy Collection)

Ginny Sims rolls out her TR 3.
(Ginny Sims Collection)

Carroll Shelby in the #98 John Edgar 410 Sport Ferrari,
Jack McAfee behind him in the 375 and assorted "track fluff"
at Palm Springs, October 1956.
(Edgar Family Collection)

Josie von Neumann in turn #3, Pomona, January 31, 1959.
(Photo: Bob Tronolone)

Ruth Levy with sometime patron
John Edgar.
(Ruth Levy Collection)

Bruce Kessler and Ruth Levy.
(Ruth Levy Collection)

Linda Scott
in a Porsche.
(Edgar Family Collection)

Ruth Levy, with Bob Bondurant's Morgan TR 2 on the tail of her
Porsche Super Speedster, at the initial Paramount Ranch races,
August 18, 1957. Ruth edged out Bob in the 20 mile race
by one second.
(Ruth Levy Collection)

Marian Lowe in her Frazer Nash Targa Florio taking a turn ahead of
Masten Gregory in a Ferrari 500 TR at Nassau, 1956.

(Photo: Tom Burnside)

Denise McCluggage stepping into a Lotus X1, Nassau, 1958.

(Bahamas News Agency)

Mary Davis, Bob Drake, Jan Harrison, Bruce Kessler on Mary's
Mercedes 300 SL with a T 39 in foreground.
(Joe Lubin Archives)

Denise McCluggage
gets a push at
Nassau, 1956.
(Photo: Tom Burnside)

Ruth Levy and
Briggs Cunningham.
(Ruth Levy Collection)

In the foreground, from left,
Formula 1 driver Jo Bonnier,
Katie Molson Moss, Ruth Levy,
hovered over by Ruth's fiancé
Ulf Norinder and Bruce Kessler.
Just above Ulf's head are
Pedro Rodriguez and
his mother.
(Ruth Levy Collection)

Linda Scott
in a Talbot Lago
F1, Pomona,
January 31, 1959.
(Photo: Bob Tronolone)

Ginny Sims in her TR 3.
(Ginny Sims Collection)

Racy home movies being shot by Porsche team manager Baron Huschke von Hanstein and starring drivers Wolfgang Seidel, Stirling Moss, Denise McCluggage, and Taffy von Trips at the Caracas Grand Prix, November 1957.
(Photo: Tom Burnside)

Ginny Sims in a Bunny car.
(Ginny Sims Collection)

Ruth Levy and
Denise McCluggage in her
trademark polka dots,
having a hoot at the
Caracas Grand Prix,
November 1957.
(Ruth Levy Collection)

Cars lined up for the Nassau Memorial Trophy Race, 1958.
(Bahamas News Agency)

Ruth Levy being treated
after crashing
Stirling Moss's borrowed
Aston Martin DBR2
at Bahamas Speed Week,
December 7, 1957.
(Ruth Levy Collection)

Ginny Sims and Mary Davis
prepare for the
Mobilgas Economy Run.
(Ginny Sims Collection)

Ginny Sims and
John von Neumann.
(Ginny Sims Collection)

Denise McCluggage and
Phil Hill at Sebring.
(Photo: Tom Burnside)

Betty Shutes (left) nipping Ruth Levy by .01 seconds in a duel of
Porsches at Pomona, February 8, 1958.
(Ruth Levy Collection)

Denise McCluggage takes the checkered flag in a ladies' race
at Nassau, 1956.
(Photo: Tom Burnside)

close behind him so photos would show its cars finishing one-two-three. What they didn't realize is that Le Mans winners are determined not by simple order of finish but by order relative to the spots where they started the race, and Ken, by easing up, had allowed the gap between him and the second car to close too much. Later that summer, he died tragically in an unexplainable accident during a practice run at Riverside.

No one was more instrumental in the growth of sports car racing in Southern California than Ken Miles. As three-term president of the California Sports Car Club during the key mid-fifties years, he oversaw event planning and the layout of new courses. Attracting enthusiasts who until then had to content themselves with small social clubs formed by like-minded workers at aircraft companies, neighborhood associations, or owners of the same brand of car, the CSCC went from crawling to walking to racing, thanks to an army of volunteers who, like the drivers, received no money and were only in it out of personal interest. A group of gearheads called the Four Cylinder Club was enlisted to oversee tech inspections at meets, and some ham radio fanatics from the One Meter Club were recruited to maintain communications during races by posting themselves at intervals around the courses and keeping officials informed of progress and problems.

In terms of getting the Cal Club on its feet and operating with some semblance of organization, the nascent Women's Sports Car Club was indispensable. From its origins, with sixteen members in September 1953, the club mushroomed to a 200-member roster within four years and essentially took over the functional operations side of CSCC events. One member in particular made it all happen—Mary Heffley. Until she was persuaded to leave her job with a manufacturer's rep by a $350-per-month offer to become secretary of the organization, the Cal Club was just feeling its way, and women in the group were, importantly, in charge of the timing and scoring of the races. Mary, who had grown up loving racing in Indiana six miles from James Dean's hometown of Fairmount (her mother and family are all buried in the same cemetery as the film star), immediately whipped the organization into shape, finding new venues, setting up regular tech inspections two nights a week, licensing drivers, and later forming a contest board to administer applications when demand grew; she still jokes about how she gave such celebrated figures as Skip Hudson and Dan Gurney their first licenses. She hired Wayne Gilson to be the club's certified public accountant, and together they prepared proper contracts with the Elks and other organizations that would help them secure new facilities. They also normalized the Cal Club's flow of revenues, which derived from gate admissions, licensing fees paid by drivers for tech inspections, and a percentage of the concessions and program advertising. (Note that the Cal Club was dealing in big money. In 1952, a driver's $20 entry fee was refundable if postmarked three weeks prior to a race and if he or she completed one lap. Accident insurance ran $8 per driver.) Operating from the big one-room office at club headquarters on Kenmore just off Hollywood Boulevard (it later moved to nearby Hillhurst in Los Feliz), Mary saw room for improvement on every front and did something about it. She bought a couple of miles' worth of snow fencing to restrain spectators, as well as a couple of tons of hay bales. She found Al Capp, a teamster who worked for the film studios and had access to any kind of equipment; when a big truck was needed to transport heavy loads to a venue, Al took care of it. Soon, Al became affectionately known as Mr. Outside, as he tended to all details of equipment and track preparations, while Mary was Miss Inside. She organized the women to cook for lunches as well as race-night barbeques, "workers' parties" that became legendary for impromptu music jams, beer consumption, pot smoking at a time before it was commonplace, and general wild times; the club was barred from the beachside Miramar Hotel after one of its members rode his motorcycle into the swimming pool. Only drivers deemed friendly by the volunteers were invited. "We had the greatest parties ever," Mary immodestly confirms. "Mardi Gras in February in Pasadena with the leftover floats from the New Year parade, summer parties, big back-room parties. We loved every minute of it." In Bill Pollack's view, "The pits at our racing venues on Saturday night resembled a casting session for a Hell's Angels movie. The beer flowed like wine. Somehow everyone survived the usual bongo marathon and, though a bit red-eyed, performed perfectly on Sunday."

Mary subsequently married driver Eric Hauser and then, with her final marriage, permanently settled on the last name of O'Connor, prompting Mary Davis to anoint her with the sobriquet Mary H2O. Despite her love of racing, Mary never truly felt the urge to join the competition herself. "I tried driving once," she allows. "I went out for a practice for a ladies' race at Pomona, in Bobby Weller's Jaguar 120. In the very next race that day, Dr. Troy Henry got killed. He ran into a tree in the backstretch. To me it was like an omen. I just didn't want to do it."

Mary remained with the Cal Club until the end of the decade, and from the 1960s until the present day she has put her extraordinary organizational skills and attention to detail to use as gatekeeper and personal majordomo for Hugh Hefner at Playboy, first in Chicago, then in Los

Angeles, where no one gets into the mansion without her knowing about it.

❑ ❑ ❑

When Josie von Neumann and her two competitors lined up at Torrey Pines for their short ladies' race in September 1951, they pushed open a door that brought on a proliferation of notable women drivers in California over the next few years. The first was Marion Lowe. The patrician Marion and her British husband, Jim, were the closest West Coast equivalents to Evelyn and John Mull; extravagantly wealthy and stylish, they lived on a magnificent ranch above Santa Cruz where they raised Aberdeen Angus cattle, and also maintained an apartment in San Francisco. They were also rather older than the young hotshots usually found around the tracks, with Marion about forty and Jim in his mid-fifties. As with the Mulls, they became interested in the sporty new European cars after World War II, and Jim gave Marion an MG TC for her birthday (while buying himself a Bentley). Wanting to give it more power, Jim sent the MG down to a shop in Long Beach, where Chuck Daigh, master mechanic and future ace driver, went to work on it, relieving it of its original engine and replacing it with a Willys Six. With this, Marion started racing, against the still-undefeated Josie von Neumann at the third Torrey Pines conclave, December 13–14, 1952. Daigh was there to watch, and will never forget the sight of Marion, in her MG TC with a Willys engine, chasing Josie and Josie spinning out in her stepfather's Porsche 356S. "Marion pulled up and stayed with her, waiting until she was ready to go again," he recalls. "When I asked her afterwards why she did that, she said, 'Well, I didn't think it would be polite to take advantage of her when she was down.'" Marion finished second in that race as a result, but had great fun racing while displaying real finesse for it in the coming years. Like most Northern California drivers, the Lowes remained more connected to the Sports Car Club of America than to the California Sports Car Club, although they moved freely around the state to race.

Marion eventually graduated to a Frazer Nash, a British sports car of which only a dozen or so were even seen in the United States; she dubbed hers "The Little Beast;" in it, she captured one of her most impressive ladies' race victories on March 21, 1954, at Minter Field near Bakersfield, beating Mary Davis and eleven others. At Santa Barbara on Labor Day weekend, 1955, she not only won the ladies' but took ninth overall and third in class in the main against the men. "It was funny because Jim had a better car but she always beat him," Daigh points out. "He was a gentleman driver, but she had more balls, she was really very good. She could go fast and never get herself in trouble, she never spun out. Most of the women I saw drive, except for Ruth Levy, their cars won the race. Marion had an average car but drove the hell out of it.

"She was just having fun, but she could have driven anything if she'd wanted to," believes Daigh who, more than fifty years later, feels that, "They were two of the best people I ever knew. Marion was a wonderful, wonderful person. There was a long road up from Route 1 to their ranch, and everyone got timed going up the hill, it was like a test drive or a hill climb. She was a wonderful cook, and they went to Europe every year to make their wine selections. One time I went to their apartment in San Francisco and she'd just gotten a Vespa motor scooter and she came out wearing a big, long, flowing white dress and asked me to hop on to take a ride. She showed me something one day, up on a big green hill. She had me lay down and look up and said, 'This is a church. You can make it anything you want.' She was one of a kind."

Another driver who stood apart from the crowd, in part because she was older than the others, was Betty Shutes. "She was, to say the least, a different fish in the pond," muses ace driver Jack McAfee, who helped Betty set up her trademark car, a Porsche 550 she brought over from Europe, and tutored her by taking her around courses and showing her how to take the lines he was using. "She wasn't a kid anymore, she owned her own car and had money. She was more a 'lady driver,' while some of the others were more hard-nosed, like Mary Davis and Ruth Levy, two of our best drivers. They'd battle you." Married to Ogden Shutes, who involved himself on the periphery of racing events from time to time, Betty was a short brunette who wore heavy makeup and painted nails, and was "very pleasant" company as far as Jack was concerned. But some of the women felt differently, especially when they started figuring out that a young lady Betty was bringing into racing was something more than just a good friend. To the other women, this helped explain why Betty kept herself apart and aloof, except on the track, where she was very competitive, often finishing in the thick of things in the women's races and winning her share of them throughout the 1950s. Betty and Mary Davis had a feud triggered by an incident during the ladies' race at Paramount Ranch on June 16, 1957, in which Mary allegedly sent Betty into a spin by bumping her from behind. Mary denies it to this day, but she was penalized by the judges who downgraded her to third place, after Ruth Levy and Beth. From then on there was no love lost between them. "I hated her and she hated me," Mary happily confesses. "She was a strange lady."

Fast, blond, and monumentally curvaceous, Mary Davis was the favorite of many male spectators; there was never any mistaking Mary on the track, what with her golden mane flying out behind her helmet like a Palomino's tail. In life she drove a circuitous route, at once precocious, taxing, and enterprising. Emotionally, she was put through the wringer. At business, she was a genius. A working-class girl who raised herself way beyond her station but always paid a price, she is a James M. Cain heroine come to life.

Cars were always a factor in her life; one killed her father in 1932, when Mary was four. Her mother, Sammy Smith, older sister Sylvia, and Mary lived at 90th Street and Central Avenue in what was, in the 1930s, a white working-class Los Angeles neighborhood about ten blocks north of Watts. For decades Sammy labored to support her girls at Firestone Rubber and Tire. After the United States entered World War II, Sylvia became a WAVE, and in 1943, when Mary was fifteen ("I didn't look it"), she decamped from Fremont High School and joined the Marines "because I wanted to have a prettier uniform than my sister. She was underage too. Our grandmother signed for both of us. Mother was okay with our joining the military. She was a very down-to-earth woman. But if I had had a daughter like me, I would have killed her."

Mary went through boot camp at Camp Lejeune in North Carolina, then was assigned to the supply depot at Isthmus Creek near San Francisco, where as a member of the Marine Corps Women's Reserve, she repaired fuel injectors for diesel engines on M4 tanks. "I loved it. It was a great experience for a kid. I thought I was growing up. My sister was decoding secret Japanese messages. They found out how old she was and wanted to keep her but they couldn't, and then they also found out how old her sister was."

When she was sixteen, in 1945, she got married—"Why, I don't know." The beau, or the culprit, as she views it now, was Bob Drake, out of the navy on a medical discharge and then, running the switchboard at the Dorchester Hotel in San Francisco. Drake, then 25, was a strange fellow, a high-spirited charmer and a scoundrel, a raffish ladies' man who was rarely known to hold down a job. "He was good at getting out of work," says Mary, who as a teenager was captivated by Drake's assurance and savvy and was easily manipulated by his glib gab. In preparation for her marriage, Mary Smith had what she imagined would be her future initials—M.D.—monogrammed on a suitcase. But, she says, Bob wouldn't let her take his name, so she changed hers to Mary Davis.

Suddenly a civilian, the underage Mary willingly took jobs Drake arranged for her, working at nightclubs and at dice games in back rooms, where the cops were paid off. Drake was, or became, a small-time pimp, developing relationships with one or two San Francisco madams. It was the perfect role for a man who always preferred to profit from someone else's hard work. Drake also liked cars. He'd raced midgets at Gilmore Stadium in Los Angeles and, like so many others, gravitated in the late 1940s to European sports cars. Mary accompanied him to the Pebble Beach races in April 1952, the second in a row won by Bill Pollack, and promptly fell in love with the MG TD. Just as Denise McCluggage had exclaimed not long before, Mary said, "I have to have it," and in 1952 bought a new one, a black-and-yellow number, at the very same showroom on Van Ness in San Francisco. "Bob was already racing. He was pretty good. I just watched at first, then I said, 'I can do that.' I had to take Drake for a ride to prove I could do it, and I did. I always came within one second of his time, on hill climbs and rallies." They started up north, then went south to Los Angeles, where Drake insisted they live separately, Mary in town, he out in Redondo Beach. But while they didn't share a domicile, they did share Mary's MG, with Bob impressing in his class in early races and Mary doing the same in ladies' events.

The couple, such as they were—Bill Pollack and others never even knew they were married—rapidly moved up in the Southern California racing world. Bob began driving Ferraris and Jaguars for Tony Parravano, and Mary soon found herself in the thick of things with the other local women; she was usually in the top three in the races she entered, and enjoyed numerous satisfying victories: at Hansen Dam, in the only race of the decade held in Los Angeles city proper, the weekend of June 18–19, 1955 in Drake's Triumph TR2 over Linda Scott and five others; at Pomona, June 23–24, 1956, where she rode her beloved 300SL to victory against heated competition from Ruth Levy, Linda Scott, Carol Givens, Ginny Sims, Betty Shutes, and seven other women; at the Del Mar Road Races, May 2–3, 1958, pushing Joe Lubin's Cooper Climax to the checkered flag ahead of Shutes in her Porsche Spyder RS, and at the fourth Hourglass running near San Diego, July 7, 1959, in Joe Lubin's 1500cc Cooper, which was then driven in the next race by Drake, who was forced to jump out of it when it caught fire. She owned, at various times, a TR2, Porsche Speedster, and Mercedes 300SL, and in some runs drove an Aston Martin, a birdcage Maserati and, her favorite, a single-seater Cooper-Climax Formula 2.

Mary was a tough competitor, and her rivalries with other women were often fierce. When Mary got to Los Angeles, Josie von Neumann essentially owned the women's races, and Mary initially found herself coming in second to Josie most of the time. Decades later, Mary still complained, only half-jokingly, that, "Josie only won because she had such damn good cars," a charge that hounded Josie throughout her career. Bill Pollack, one of the few who got to know Josie fairly well, liked her and found her "a sweet person," but was less taken with her automotive skills. "She was just okay," he found. "She did have an advantage. John built that MG for her that was super-light and very competitive. You could have put almost anybody in that car and it would do well. I'm not sure she ever got more than seventy-five to eighty percent out of that car." Bruce Kessler agrees, stressing, "She drove equipment that was not available to other people. Honestly, Josie would never have stood up in other competition. She drove when there was no competition." Mary respected her, but there was never any rapport between them and one can only imagine how the squat, glum-looking Josie felt when dazzling, golden Mary suddenly showed up on the scene.

Mary was at Torrey Pines on July 10, 1955, when the only female fatality in California sports car racing history took place. A little-known driver named Margaret

Pritchard entered the ladies race that day. Driving an ugly-looking homemade vehicle with a Plymouth or Dodge V-8 engine, Pritchard came much too fast out of the first curve, spun out, and turned over. She evidently died instantly, although the race continued and was won by Josie von Neumann. Pritchard's husband was a navy man away at sea, and all the racers were aghast thinking of how he would have to be notified of his wife's death. Coming as it did exactly one month after the scores of fatalities at Le Mans, the accident raised serious hackles in Sacramento, where some politicians made noises about banning or seriously restricting race car driving in California, but this eased up soon enough. Max Balchowsky, owner of Hollywood Motors and an accomplished auto modifier, subsequently acquired the crashed car, reconfigured it and rechristened it "Ole Yeller" (sometimes written "Ol' Yaller"), in which guise it became a well-known winner in the hands of Eric Hauser, Mary O'Connor's husband at the time.

The following year, Mary Davis, Bob Drake, and Dan Gurney became part of a team put together by Joe Lubin, a new entrant who had made his money in heavy equipment and junk dealing and had recently become a Cooper importer. "Joe was very wealthy, a very nice man, really wonderful," proclaims Mary. "He took all our trophies for his kids." It was in Lubin's new Cooper T39 "Bobtail" that Drake, a hard-charging driver who was often in contention, scored perhaps his greatest victory, over heavy competition in the November 1956 SCCA National in Palm Springs.

All this time, Bob Drake had diddled around with various small-time business ventures, including running a charter deep-sea fishing-boat concern, but dedicated himself to having a good time. "Everybody loved the guy," Mary wearily admits. "Bob had a great sense of humor, everyone thought he was so charming. They all thought, 'Good old Bob,' 'Life-of-the-party Bob.' But they didn't know him behind closed doors, they didn't know his dark side. Bob would go to the Coach and Horses"— the rowdy Sunset Boulevard bar where the young racing crowd convened—"but he wouldn't take me. He chippied all the time." Another woman driver and Mary's best friend, Ginny Sims, saw enough to realize that "Bob Drake was Jekyll and Hyde." Bob often squired around another woman, a redhead known to the crowd only as Judy, who was rumored to have once been a working girl up in San Francisco. What she was doing sharing motel rooms with Bob and Mary on trips to out-of-town races was much speculated upon, but no one asked for details.

Life with Drake became torture for Mary. She wanted out, but was paralyzed from fear of what he might do if she tried to leave. So like the heroine of a Hollywood melodrama from the period who, done wrong by her man, figures out that she can only succeed by looking out for herself, Mary looked her problems straight in the eye and made herself into a businesswoman. She enrolled in Lumlow Real Estate School and then took a job with Beth Properties in West Hollywood, where she was an instant success, selling homes all over Los Angeles.

The Coach and Horses, a divey bar on Sunset Boulevard near Stanley that is still in business, was presided over at the time by a genuine character who went by the name of "High School" Harry Givens, so named, it was said, because he liked high-school girls. His predelictions notwithstanding, High School Harry did have a wife, Carol, and they both raced, in their own fashion. As Bill Pollack remembers it, Harry "drove a Jaguar like he was trying out for the demoliton derby. The car was always sideways, even in the pit." Confounding all the drivers, Harry, who was an average-looking guy, outdid them all when it came to women. He had a boat, and fifty years later Pollack still can't get over how, when he'd visit, "One of Harry's several ex-wives would be present along with a current wife and at least one girlfriend."

The scene at the Coach and Horses was thick with drivers plus an overlap of Hollywood gearheads. Phil Hill, Carroll Shelby, Jack McAfee, James Dean, Steve McQueen and many others hung out there, doing lots of serious drinking and pranking. "It was an unbelievable place," remembers Bruce Kessler, a car-mad Beverly Hills rich boy whose mother was the prime mover behind Rosemarie Reid, the swimwear line that swept the country in the late 1940s. Kessler and his best friend Lance Reventlow, son of Woolworth heiress Barbara Hutton and the Danish count Kurt Haugwitz Hardenberg Reventlow, sometimes filled in as bartenders, even though both of them were distinctly under drinking age—they had been born a month apart in 1936. Kessler pulled the same stunt at the track, entering the January 23–24, 1954 Palm Springs event with a phony I.D. He finished second in his Jag in the over-1500cc race, but when officials discovered he was only seventeen, he was suspended for the 1955 season.

At the Coach and Horses, Kessler remembers, "Sometimes we'd take over behind the bar at two A.M., which was closing time, and serve drinks until three for free. If you wanted food, you went into the refrigerator and helped yourself and left whatever you thought it was worth.

"It was an off-the-wall place. It had a number of alkie regulars, but lots of weird characters came in too. In those days, people didn't flaunt their sexual preferences, or talk about whether they were gay or lesbians. One night, these two girls in leather came in, and Lance said something to one of them, and a helluva fight broke out.

They had to be separated. She could really punch. Lance offended a dyke, so there was a big, big fight."

In 1956, blossoming real-estate magnate Mary Davis had a brainstorm she shared with Bob, Harry, and Carol. Given all the people they knew, was there not great potential for a legitimate restaurant and watering hole with an auto-racing bent? They agreed, especially since they knew Mary was going to raise all the money and make it happen. And that she did. Taking over a corner site formerly occupied by Ken's Hula Hut, at 8204 Beverly Boulevard, Mary oversaw everything, from the contracting and menu to hiring an artist from Marymount College named Pauline Kouri to create large automotive paintings for the walls. Bob was to serve as host, and High School Harry would tend bar. So was the Grand Prix born.

From the moment the doors opened on Valentine's Day, 1957, the place was a great success. Serving lunch and dinner, it offered juicy steaks, potent cocktails, bench racing, and free racing movies projected every Tuesday, Thursday, and Saturday night. Advertisements conveyed the desired tone via a photograph of the hosts, Bob and Mary, seated in hot race cars. Their many friends became loyal regulars, Cal Club meetings were held there, Hollywood folk came by, and it became an essential destination for out-of-town car personalities visiting Los

Angeles. Its popular nickname was the "Grand Pricks," "appropriately enough," in Mary's view, "considering some of our customers."

But there was trouble in this little paradise. According to Mary, "Carol decided to rip us off, so they both had to go, she and Harry. I put up all the money, but she decided she was going to steal it." Mary practically lived at the Grand Prix, and only she was responsible enough to make sure everything was tended to. "Drake would come in every morning and take twenty dollars out of the box. He was taking money for himself." In the end, a strong melancholy shadowed her outstanding business accomplishment. "The only reason I went into it was so that Bob would have something successful so I could get away from him," she admits. Instead, he was now on a gravy train that gave him more reason than ever to keep Mary in his life. Mary would be forced to orchestrate an even grander scheme to rid herself of the Svengali who had become a leech.

Mary's best friend Ginny Sims is an excellent example of a professional working woman for whom auto racing made life exceptional. Born Ginny Jeffers in Los Angeles in 1920 to a family with California roots that predate statehood, she remembers her father taking her to races at Beverly Hills' long-extinct board racetrack as a babe-in-arms, and later was able to walk from home to

Gilmore Field, next to the Farmer's Market, to see midget racing. "I was so independent," she reflects. "When my parents gave me my roller skates, I was off. That was their first mistake, giving me a set of wheels."

Ginny's father, who had a carburetor equipment company at Fifteenth and Hill in Los Angeles, taught his daughter to drive in a Model A when she was eleven, on old dirt roads out in the San Fernando Valley. Tall, statuesque, and with twinkly blue eyes, Ginny was twenty when, on an outing with her family to Griffith Park, she spotted a young fellow working under the hood of a hot rod at the Hammy's Hamburgers lot. "I said, 'Who's the big guy down there?' It was Frank Sims, holder of a UCLA degree in geology and former football player, three years Ginny's senior. They married quickly, but were soon separated by the war and scarcely saw each other for more than three years. Frank joined the army and ended up in India, on the Burma Road and in China, while Ginny became a WAVE; she hung engines on planes at Alameda, where her best memory is of a friend flying her in a Grumman F-4 two-seater under the Bay Bridge, and was later stationed in New York City and Washington, D.C. Her daughter Fran was born in 1945, but after the war, Frank's new job as a troubleshooter for Standard Oil took him overseas again. The strain of constant separation was finally too much, and they split two years later. "We went our separate ways," Ginny says, "but he was the best." Ginny married at twenty, again at thirty, and a final time at forty, making a point not to make the mistake again at her four subsequent decade milestones.

Ginny started itching to do something shortly after marrying her second husband, small-time actor William Meader, who, according to Ginny, had been run out of New York for fooling around with a mobster's girl and now worked mostly as Fredric March's stand-in. She asked a union-official friend if he could help get her into the union so she could get a job in films. "He asked, 'Aren't you happy being a housewife?' and I said, 'Hell, no!'" She went to work at Technicolor in 1951 writing down edge numbers, a monotonous job in the film-editing field that was the first step on a road that eventually led to Ginny becoming head of negative cutting at Paramount.

When she was with Frank, the couple would go up to Muroc and Rosamond Dry Lakes, beyond Lancaster, a popular weekend destination for hot-rodders in the 1940s, where they'd sleep in the car and racing would start at sunup. Or they might venture to Saugus to watch old-time racers. But when Ginny started meeting some of the car crowd at the Coach and Horses and watching the racing home movies there, she decided she had to hit the track herself. "That's how I got into racing," she said. She started in 1956 with an MG TD, trading in an old Hudson she called "The Brown Badoodoo." The MG was white, with red upholstery, "the cutest thing you ever saw. I loved that little car."

More women tended to race in Santa Barbara than at any other track, and that's where, in April 1956, Ginny began. She handled herself well, moving from last up to fifth in her first ladies' race. On a later visit to Santa Barbara, where, after five or six more races, she admittedly still didn't feel she knew what she was doing, Bob Drake gave Ginny a crucial master class in racing by walking the entire track with her and Mary. "Nobody had ever done that for me," she said. "He explained the line to take through a corner, where to gear down, how wide to take the turns, when to put your foot in it. You got refined."

Suddenly, Ginny found, "Racing was my every weekend thing. I'd take my daughter and she had her fun there and fell in with other sons and daughters." The only bump in the road was an unexpected piece of publicity highlighting her growing success. When she had bought her new car, Ginny had allayed her mother's suspicions by lying that she wasn't racing. "I thought if my mother had known about it, she would have died. It was a secret. Then the *Times* ran a big picture of me, and she called and said, 'I thought you weren't racing!' My father was okay with it, though."

She was a solid, even strong driver, although she didn't push it the way Mary or Josie did. "I never wanted to get that dirty," she says. "I just wanted to drive." Deciding she needed a more powerful car, Ginny's mechanic Ted Swindun recommended a Triumph TR3, so she got a white one and won a couple of races in it. This got her invitations to drive other people's cars. Specifically, John Edgar came calling, something many others dreamed might happen, but not Ginny. "He wanted me to drive a Ferrari. He was such a pain in the butt, calling up all the time at two in the morning. I started getting butterflies, stomach trouble. I had a daughter to raise and a job to do. Ruth Levy drove for him."

As well as anyone, Ginny epitomized the Southern California woman driver who raced because she loved it, was sufficiently obsessed to do it every weekend, and got so much out of her comparatively brief involvement that it has sustained her social life and memory bank ever since. She also recognized her limits. As Bill Pollack puts it, "Ginny would never get in a car she didn't feel she could handle. Ginny and Mary Davis were similar in that neither would ever wreck a car. But Ginny drove with some degree of precaution, while Mary was almost as ballsy as Ruth Levy. She was a risk-taker in racing and in real life. If Mary were a twenty-year-old today, she'd probably be headed for Indy."

Another top woman driver and a popular favorite was, like Mary and Ginny, a native of Los Angeles, but conspicuously from the other side of town. Linda Scott was raised comfortably in Los Angeles's upscale Brentwood district and went to a rigorous Catholic school. In high school she met both future star driver Richie Ginther and Bill Scott, whom she married and with whom she bought an MG TD and started running in Cal Club meets in the mid-1950s.

Five decades later, everybody in Southern California car circles, man or woman, lights up at the mention of her name and remembers her for three things: her looks, her speed, and her favorite car. In a milieu not lacking in attractive women, Linda still stood out. A tall and slim girl with sandy blond hair and a feel for fashion, Linda looked like a *Vogue* covergirl and was approached about modeling and film work but wasn't interested; she knew that world through her grandfather, silent-screen star Francis X. Bushman, and it held little appeal.

Her future lay almost entirely with machines and speed. By 1956 she was showing promise in ladies' races at the usual Los Angeles-area venues, and on December 8, 1957, she scored her first important victory, piloting an A.C.-Bristol to the finish line at Paramount Ranch ahead of perennial rivals Mary Davis and Betty Shutes. This brought her to the attention of Otto Zipper, a wealthy Beverly Hills Porsche dealer whose ties to the von Neumann family dated back to prewar Vienna. He was now active as an entrant, with Ken Miles as his main driver. Looking for a woman who could do well in the ladies' races, Zipper took Linda on, and she drove for him for a couple of years in a Porsche RSK. But the car in his collection that really interested her was an oddity on the circuit, and a car no one had seen a woman handle successfully before: a 1949 single-seat Talbot-Lago T26 Grand Prix edition, with a 4.5-liter six-cylinder engine. An open-wheeled, cigar-shaped silver tube with exhaust pipes that dramatically peeled out from under the hood and ran along the car's extreme eight-foot wheelbase, the Talbot was a noisy beauty, powerful but not quite as fast as some subsequently built racers. It was also heavy and stiff, "a very complex thing to drive," Bill Pollack testifies. As an old GP car, it wasn't allowed in normal class events, so instead, Linda drove the Talbot in Formula Libre races, where anything went. This enabled her to compete against top male drivers from time to time; one of her most memorable races in the Talbot had her in the thick of things and finally finishing fourth at Riverside in 1958 against an array of very fast cars driven by the likes of Ginther, John von Neumann, Lance Reventlow, Bob

Oker, and Pete Woods. She stopped racing the following year because of her pregnancy with her first child, and never went back when it became clear that her kind of racing was suddenly a thing of the past.

Sizing up the involvement of women in sports car racing in the early 1950s, Pollack believes that the Cal Club—the way it was set up and evolved—provided an ideal way for women to enter racing and find their own levels. "Up until the Cal Club, I don't find in any other sport a situation where women could come in and compete as a group. It was very much open in L.A. I think the Cal Club was the first place to offer the women their own races, and in this way they could earn the respect of the men so they could eventually drive in any race. It was a chance to show the guys that they could do it too."

Linda Scott, who joined the Cal Club in the mid-1950s, preferred the "looser" attitude at the local organization to the "very clubby atmosphere" that prevailed at the Sports Car Club of America. Ignazio E. Lozana Jr., contest board representative of the SCCA, explained the club's approach to women's racing to Evelyn Mull at the time: "We have no specific rule barring women from racing with the men. In fact, no woman who holds a current competition license has ever been refused. However, there are several reasons why so few women race with men in this region. One, we always schedule a women's event in every race program. This is to accommodate the women as well as the men, since most of the women realize that they have not the skill or the urge to compete with men on even terms, and the better men drivers feel that their normal verve (of which we have an abundance) is somewhat inhibited when they realize that the driver of the car which they are about to chop off may be someone's mother.

"Two, most of our women drivers are not members of the club, but rather wives of members. Therefore they cannot hold competition licenses. They are subjected to the same tests as men—written exam, physical exam, and driving tests.

"Three, very few of our women drivers have a car to drive during the men's races, since they are usually being driven by a man in those events. Should we discontinue the ladies' races, it would mean we would have at the most two or three women drivers in our program, whereas in the ladies' races we have had as many as twenty-five starters."

Much as he liked and admired the women who raced sports cars in the 1950s and was pleased to welcome them as competitors, Bill Pollack speaks for many of the men when he makes what he views as one important distinction between the sexes on the track: "I always detected a small seed of fear in women drivers. Often guys have qualms before a big race, but maybe they can hide it better. At least as it happened at that time, if there's a situation in racing that's dangerous, guys are more likely to take that shot than women. Women by nature are more conservative about safety, they are not going to be foolish and reckless. Ninety-eight percent of the people, men and women, in the Cal Club were club drivers. Josie and Mary and Ginny were very good club drivers. Two percent were guys like Phil Hill, myself, Carroll Shelby. We could go for it."

Bill and the rest of the guys were about to meet someone who would give the women their 2 percent.

WHIRLWIND FROM THE NORTH

Women aren't supposed to drive that fast.

—MARION LOWE

It was on January 29, 1956, in the depths of a Minnesota winter, that American network television put a camera on a female race car driver for the first time. It was not an auspicious occasion, although it must have seemed like a good idea at the time, at least to Dave Garroway, a car nut who decided to spotlight a winner of the previous year's St. Paul Winter Carnival Ice Race on his NBC show *Wide Wide World*. Ruth Levy was such an engaging and chatty young lady that she seemed like a natural to provide a running commentary on the race while driving in her new, snow-white Porsche Speedster convertible, top down, and she readily agreed. After being elaborately wired with an airplane pilotlike headset and

213

mouthpiece, she zoomed off the starting line and proceeded to run her car straight into a snowbank; after regaining her composure, she still managed to finish second in Class F. Although the embarrassing accident was actually a precursor of a worse moment to come, Ruth's spectacular farewell to ice racing was hardly representative of her brief but blazing racing days.

"Balls out" is how more than one competitor have described her approach to driving. "Fearless, very daring," comments McCluggage. "Pushing the limits all the time," says Kessler. "A very heavy foot, just like Kessler," observes Pollack. It was a half century ago that Ruth Levy took the California racing scene by storm, but people there still talk about her. She's one of the main reasons the fifties were fabulous.

It wasn't always easy, especially toward the beginning, but Ruth has led several amazing lives. "I love my life," she says. "It's a great story, and I couldn't have done it without my parents." Her maiden name isn't Levy but Cohen, and not even that, really; she was adopted shortly after her birth in New York City on October 29, 1930, by Jacob "Jack" and Teresa Cohen; a boy, David, had been adopted the previous year. Jack Cohen was a successful publisher of medical journals, beginning with a dental magazine, achieved a national profile with *Modern Medicine* and ultimately added eight more journals under the banner. He was a prominent and influential figure in Minneapolis and motivated his children in learning and culture. He encouraged books and art—Ruth later studied at the Minneapolis Institute of Art, and Dad bought all her paintings—but Ruth developed a strong interest in sports, taking to touch football, ice racing, and ice boating with her brother, with whom she was always driven to "keep up." She also rode horses and swam for her school.

"I remember all our cars," Ruth asserts. "My dad had a thirty-five-acre farm out of town, and out there we had a 'thirty-nine Buick with suicide doors and a farm truck and a tractor. I ran the tractor into the barn. Dad had a 'forty-one Packard Coupé de Luxe, and Mom later had a 'forty-seven Buick Roadster. Dad tried to teach us to drive, but after a week he turned us over to a guy from the Auto Club. For a week I only drove backwards, and then he pushed his foot down; I was driving, but he kept applying his foot to mine, going faster and faster, until I could handle the turning."

Ruth was thankful for the lively household in which she grew up, but also appreciated "the boys from the gas station"—guys like Chris Tanida, who ran the Shell station; Don Skogmo, a rich kid who loved fast cars and was killed years later racing at Elkhart Lake; future club driver Zane Mann; and John Barless. "I didn't have a lot of girlfriends, but all the guys I hung out with worked in garages and raced cars through alleys." At one point she got a scholarship to attend art school in Paris, but her father wanted her to stay and get married. "It was not what I wanted to do. If I was going to get married, I really wanted to marry Skogmo," Ruth allows. "But Dad wanted me to marry a nice Jewish boy, and I loved my dad. I married only to please my dad." So where did Ruth go to find herself the right fellow? Where else but the Flame, a Minneapolis bar where she met jazz pianist Lou Levy. Just twenty-one, Levy was already a recognized up-and-comer, having accompanied Sarah Vaughan in his native Chicago and having recently joined Woody Herman's celebrated Four Brothers band. The latter was well known for its consumption of illegal substances, but Ruth, at nineteen, was oblivious to this for more than a while. "I said, 'He's a nice Jewish piano player. Is that okay, Dad?'"

At first, she was sustained by the exhilaration of early 1950s New York City, where Lou had a gig; the night life, hanging out with the musicians, becoming pregnant. But then the realities of the road became oppressive, finally impossible—"hookers and junkies in hideous hotels—it was great," snorts Ruth, with one, then two little daughters in tow. For a long time, Lou hid his drug habit from his wife. "He pretended he had the flu," she says.

"But they were all shooting up." By 1954, the marriage was over. Eventually overcoming his addiction, Lou went on to a shimmering career as the preferred piano accompanist of Stan Getz, Frank Sinatra, Ella Fitzgerald, Lena Horne, Peggy Lee, and Nancy Wilson. He was a bop-influenced musician with a style so smooth and singer-intuitive he was nicknamed the "Silver Fox."

Fortunately, Ruth had her family to fall back on. Living at the farm outside Minneapolis, she reconnected with the garage boys and bought an MG TC. But she and her parents were still suffering from the loss of Ruth's gregariously athletic older brother David, who was killed in Korea. David's death, however, provided Ruth with an unanticipated stepping-stone to her future; receiving $10,000 from her brother's army insurance policy, she spent a third of it when, on a trip to New York with her younger sister, she impulsively decided to buy a Porsche Speedster from Max Hoffman's showroom, then drove it back to Minnesota. Echoing the words of so many others who experienced love at first sight with a car, she says, "When I saw it, I knew I had to have it." Wistfully, Ruth speculates, "If my brother hadn't been killed, we probably both would have raced cars."

After her startling victory in the January 1955 Ice Race, Ruth, Skogmo, who that year won the main race for the second time in a row, and one or two of the other guys decided to give it a go in some regional SCCA Midwestern races that summer; in her beloved Porsche, she finished sixth in the under-1500cc event and first against twelve others in the ladies' at Iowa City on May 30, third at Milwaukee, and, amazingly, fifth against an otherwise all-male lineup at Elkhart Lake, including Phil Hill. All this was enough to put some wild ideas in her head. How she talked her mother into it is hard to fathom, as Mom, thinking of Ruth's daughters, pushed for Ruth to get married again. But Ruth convinced her it was essential that she follow her passion for racing to California, and Mom agreed to babysit the girls for six weeks while Ruth got organized.

In April 1956, Ruth drove alone in the Porsche across the Rockies, where she ran smack into a fierce late-season blizzard; "It was the only time I had the top up." The Speedster had no defroster, only a heater in the floorboard, so Ruth jerry-rigged a radiator hose up to the windshield with duct tape. Upon arriving in Los Angeles, the Porsche, as if equipped with radar, somehow honed in directly on the Coach and Horses, where Ruth was instantly adopted by High School Harry and Carol Givens. "The place was insane," says Ruth, who couldn't have been more at home. "Lance Reventlow, Bruce Kessler, the young Hollywood pretty set, the best hamburgers, full of photos of everybody that had raced.

We'd tell jokes and laugh and laugh." One afternoon Ava Gardner came in for a drink, and that night Harry auctioned off the glass she drank from and the barstool she sat on. Sometimes, when everyone was good and drunk, the revelers would indulge in a special indoor sport called "walking the ledge." A thin ledge ran along the length of the high wall above the bar down to the phone booth at the end of the room, and the challenge was to climb up above the booth and walk the ledge to the front. "I did it twice, but facing the wall," Ruth admits. "Then they made me turn around. I looked down and said, 'Get me off of here!'"

Practically overnight, everyone in town knew about Ruth. Along with the drivers at Coach and Horses, the ball of fire with short dark hair started hanging out at John von Neumann's Competition Motors on Cahuenga and dated his mechanic, the odd and unstable Rolf Wuetherich. The moody, dark-haired German was still recovering from the frightful injuries he suffered while riding passenger in James Dean's new 550 Spyder, nicknamed "Little Bastard," on their way to races in Salinas on September 30, 1955. The day had started at von Neumann's shop where the car was prepared and while waiting Dean had lunch at the Farmer's Market. On the way north, Dean spotted Bruce Kessler driving Lance Reventlow's Mercedes 300SL and they pulled over for a break. In the late afternoon Dean and Wuetherich were approaching the intersection of Routes 466 and 41 at Cholame when a college student named Donald Turnupseed, going the other way, made a left turn in front of the Porsche. In one of Wuetherich's accounts, Dean's last words were, "That guy up there's gotta stop; he'll see us." At another time, the mechanic confessed to having been dozing just before the accident. In all events, the impact threw Wuetherich, who wasn't wearing a seat belt, out of the car, while Dean, who was strapped in, was mortally injured, his chest crushed and head nearly severed from his body.

Although there was always skepticism among the race crowd about actors who suddenly decided they were hot drivers, Dean looked like the genuine article. He only raced for one short season. At Palm Springs, on March 26, 1955, he drove the Porsche Speedster he'd bought from von Neumann to victory in the six-lap novice race—required of first-timers—and the next day startled everyone by taking third place in the 27-lap under-1500cc main event behind Ken Miles and Cy Yedor. At an SCAA National event at Minter Field near Bakersfield on April 30, Dean took first in Class F and third overall in the production car race, and the next day he finished ninth overall and second in class in the under-1500cc main against formidable competition. In Santa

Barbara on May 29, he had moved from eighteenth place up to fourth before a mechanical failure forced him out. Although most of the drivers found him taciturn and standoffish, Dean hung out in the pits for a long time with Josie von Neumann in Santa Barbara and expressed the hope, before heading off to film *Giant*, to one day win a Grand Prix race in a Maserati.

When Ruth met Wuetherich about eight months after the crash, he was still on crutches and was suffering physically and mentally. "He had great tenacity, the will to pull himself through it. But he was haunted. He didn't want to talk about Dean or the accident," says Ruth. "He was really tormented, and he was constantly hounded by the press." Fate had spared Wuetherich on that September 30 but came for him in July 1981, when he ran his car off the road in Germany and slammed into a house, apparently while drunk. Eerily, the first California race Ruth attended was at Pebble Beach on April 22, 1956, when the so well liked Ernie McAfee fatally rammed into a tree, signaling the end of racing at the fabled road course and the switch to the purpose-built Laguna Seca nearby the following year.

Death was always lurking nearby during those years, in sports car racing just as in Formula 1, although it wasn't something drivers talked about, for fear of engendering a ban on the growing sport they loved. The first Cal Club member to die driving was Bill Powell, who was killed in a Saturday practice at Willow Springs on February 12, 1955. On October 20 of the following year, Dr. Troy McHenry perished in his new fiberglass-bodied, Porsche 550-powered special. But the worst was to come, at Paramount Ranch the weekend of December 7–8, 1957. In the Saturday practice, Hugh Woods ran his Corvette into the guardrail at the end of the main straightaway, losing his right leg and suffering multiple fractures. Later that day, in the over-2700cc race, Robert Sheppard died at almost precisely the same spot when he evidently missed a downshift in his XK120 Jag at the end of the straight, veered onto the turf and uncontrollably shot across the turn toward the rail. Despite this, the Sunday races proceeded as planned, allowing Linda Scott her long-awaited victory in the ladies' event. In the main, Dan Gurney in Frank Arciero's 4.9 Ferrari had already taken the checkered flag when Jim Firestone in a Frazer-Nash, evidently affected by a gust of wind, lost control and crashed in the underpass, where he died. Lloyd's canceled its insurance, and this was the last public sports car race day at Paramount Ranch.

One of Ruth's new friends from the Coach and Horses was self-described "Hollywood playguy" Bill Gardner, an actors' manager, publicist, and social fixer who knew everybody. A rowdy Irishman who, like Ruth, hailed from Minnesota, he managed Mickey Rooney and Jonathan Winters, ran with guys like Robert Mitchum and John Huston, loved a good time and tried to make sure everyone else had one too. He also helped bring the racing and film crowds closer together when he started throwing big parties in Palm Springs at the Desert Inn, where he worked for the hotel's owner, Hearst "widow" Marion Davies.

Within a month of her arrival in California, on May 19 to be precise, Ruth made her racing debut in the state, at Minter Field outside Bakersfield. When she pulled up in her Porsche, she was approached by the imposing Jack McAfee, who said, " 'So you're the lady hotshot driver from Minnesota?' I said, 'Okay,' and I thought, What an asshole. Of course, we became great buds." Although well aware of the scrutiny she was under, Ruth felt no anxiety before her California debut; as always, she knew she was just going to go for it. In the ladies' event, Ruth's well-traveled "white bathtub," as she called her Porsche, gave Mary Davis in her Mercedes 300SL a hard run to finish second; the next day, she took fourth in class as the only woman in an over-1500cc stock and modified production contest.

The weekend marked the beginning of a hot rivalry between Ruth and Mary that repeatedly played itself out on the track over the next two years. As the two gutsiest women on the circuit, they were very competitive as drivers; Ruth won more often than not, but Mary could keep up with her. Of all the rivalries in women's racing, it was theirs that became physical. One memorable night some time later at the Grand Prix, Ruth was at a booth with Bill Gardner when Mary had words with her. "Right away, I could tell the sparks were going to fly," Gardner remembers. "They really got into it, and there was a cat fight. They both got in some hits." Ruth says, "All I remember is getting tangled up on an ocean of blond hair. And I was asked not to come back to the Grand Prix." The women eventually got over it and remained friendly rivals, but rivals all the same, until decades later, when they finally established a mutual understanding and fine rapport.

More small meets followed, leading up to the opening of a new course at an old San Fernando Valley movie location, the Paramount Ranch, on August 18–19, 1956. The twisty, hilly run quickly gained a reputation as a real "driver's course," and was arguably the most beautiful in Southern California, with its thickly wooded glades, central lake, and over-and-underpasses. Ruth loved the course, saying "it makes racers out of drivers, drivers of novices and chickens of the spectators." Ruth proceeded to prove herself a real racer there, handily defeating Linda Scott in the ladies' and finishing first in class E; at weekend's close, she ranked eleventh overall.

By the time Mom turned up with little Jackie and Pam, Ruth had found herself a secluded place up Tiger Tail Road north of Sunset in Brentwood for $220 a month. As soon as she had lined up a tag team of UCLA girls to babysit in shifts, she was off to the races. To greater or lesser extents, all these women who raced forfeited something important to drive competitively, and it invariably involved family. A generation before "career versus family" became a sociopolitical football, these women were confronted with choices about what they would give up to follow their passion. And it was only for passion and fun and self-realization that they made their sacrifice, not for a career or financial gain. In percentages far higher than the norm, they did not have children, and if they did, there were emotional problems or estrangement; the marriages were often strained, and almost universally there was divorce; only the extravagantly wealthy Marion Lowe and Elizabeth/Isabelle Haskell, among the prominent drivers, had the same husband from youth to old age. This can't be a complete coincidence. The benign description of the fast women is that they were free spirits; the traditionalist view would harp on selfishness and irresponsibility, at least if there were kids involved. The women have not expressed regrets publicly and in interviews said they wouldn't be who they are without racing; the activity defines them, just as any sport defines its devotees. As these women saw it, they had no choice. At the very least, it seemed like the most important thing at the time.

"Ruth made a big impression when she got here," observes California racing historian Jim Sitz, who saw her in action. "She embarrassed guys." Nonetheless, Ruth hit a bit of a rut toward the end of 1956, exemplified by her somewhat disappointing showing in the eagerly anticipated climax of the fall season, the first SCCA National Championship races at the Palm Springs airport course. The weekend of November 3–4 was everything everyone could have wanted it to be and more, on both the racing and social sides. In one-hundred-degree heat, Carroll Shelby showed off John Edgar's Ferrari 4.1—"the best car I ever drove," the crafty Texan said—to brilliant advantage in taking the main event, a victory that became legendary in part because he had been up partying the entire night before. His competition included Phil Hill, just back from a successful European season, in a Monza 3.5, Bill Murphy in a Kurtis-Buick, Bob Drake in a Joe Lubin Aston Martin, and Jack McAfee in John Edgar's Porsche 550 Spyder. On the women's side, Marion Lowe proved there was iron beneath her well-mannered façade, going wire-to-wire to beat Mary Davis in a TR-3 and Ruth in her suddenly insufficient-looking Speedster.

Whereas the airport had to shut down for a time to accommodate the races (a scheduled commercial flight landed promptly at 4:30 P.M. on Sunday, just fifteen minutes after the last race ended), the partying continued on a virtual twenty-four-hour basis. Saturday evening's Biltmore bash, the one Carroll Shelby never left, lasted all night. Will Edgar, just out of the air force and accompanying his wife and triumphant dad, describes the climactic celebrations evocatively: "I still feel the night and how it went in a moving feast from victory banquet at the Oasis Hotel to the Palm Springs Biltmore, Okanu's bongo drums, tequila in every glass, Bill Gardner corralling his party friends, the men and women, the singing and dancing. Federico Fellini might have staged it all for his cameras at Rome's Cinecittà."

◘ ◘ ◘

From a bacchanalian point of view, Palm Springs was just a rehearsal for what took place a month later in the Bahamas. Uncharacteristically, Ruth Levy wasn't there; she was busy becoming engaged to Charles "Chuckles" Rosher, son of the famous Hollywood cameraman of the same name and future cinematographer himself but then a good-times boy and celebrated prankster whose mother wanted him to have nothing to do with race cars. Will Edgar was a classmate at Harvard Military School and remembers Rosher as "crazy fun. He was a real cut-up there. He raised hell."

Just about anyone who could finagle a ride, and even some who weren't entirely sure what car they might be driving, managed to show up in Nassau during the first two weeks of December 1956. As an event officially sponsored by the Fédération Internationale de l'Automobile, it drew a healthy representation of top international drivers, and as an offshore venue close to the United States, it was alluring to American amateur sports car racers for its convenience, glamour, and lack of restrictions over participation. It was, in short, a great opportunity for Yank and foreign drivers to mix it up.

Originally conceived by the Trade Development Board as a way to spark hotel business during the dormant pre-Christmas period, the event, formally dubbed the Nassau Trophy Road Races but properly called The Bahamas Speed Week, was organized by Captain Sherman F. ("Red") Crise and enthusiastically supported by reigning local aristocrats Sir Sydney and Lady Oakes, not only as backers but drivers. As the races were preceded by a week of cocktail parties, which then increased in number on the weekend of actual competition, the good-times priorities of the organizers could not have been clearer. A special boat was arranged to bring the cars over to the island, and even their unloading provided great excitement among the locals in what was one of the last outposts of the traditional British colonialism.

Upon checking in to Nancy Oakes's recently refurbished British Colonial Hotel, drivers and other guests were given a program listing all the parties they were encouraged to attend and a lapel button to gain them admittance. The nightlife, pursued at such boîtes as the Junkanoo Club, the Pilot House Club, and most popularly, Dirty Dick's Bar, was raucous and highly lubricated. The calypso bands, then an international sensation, were terrific, and the women fabulous even by high race-world standards; outsiders were knowledgeably informed that the blondes, nicknamed "Snow Whites," were the general preference of Maserati and Ferrari drivers, while Mercedes and Porsche men were more inclined toward brunettes.

The racing, which was frequently delayed and even more often conducted with serious hangovers, took place on the Windsor Road Race Course, a three-and-a-half-mile run marked out by oil cans and sand dunes over a former air base then being converted into Nassau's main airport. The racing surface, a mix of asphalt and crushed coral, was murder on tires. This was the event's third year. In 1954, there had been a limited array of races, and Masten Gregory, the thin, handsome, drawling Kansan, and

Spain's aristocratic playboy Alfonso de Portago, both in Ferraris, had dominated the main races. Things expanded considerably in 1955, with de Portago and Phil Hill finishing one-two in the thirty-lap Governor's Trophy race and the same drivers reversing those positions in the climactic, sixty-lap Nassau Trophy race, with Gregory third and Isabelle Haskell, the only woman on record as having competed, twenty-first.

In 1956, Speed Week grew ever more ambitious and popular; there would be fourteen events overall, including a locals' race (won, curiously enough, by event chairman Red Crise) as well as, for the first time, two ladies' heats, which got women to Nassau in sizeable numbers. The lineup of international drivers was formidable. Climaxing an extraordinary year in which he knocked off nineteen victories in a row at one stretch, Carroll Shelby was attending for the first time, as were Jim Kimberly and Lance Reventlow. Gregory, Hill, and de Portago would be back; John Fitch and Ken Miles were signed on, and best of all, Stirling Moss, the most exciting young racer in the world, was flying in all the way from Melbourne, Australia, for the main.

Shelby made his trip worthwhile by racking up another victory, driving Edgar's Ferrari 410 S in the Governor's Trophy race over de Portago. Both ladies' events, which involved nine participants battling it out over five laps, took place on December 8, and it is best to let Denise McCluggage describe it the way she reported it to her readers of the *Herald Tribune*, as a first-person account of her pre-race travails.

> Now for the women's races. It was almost a race to see how many cars I could almost drive. Bill Lloyd's three-litre Maserati, which I was originally going to drive, was in an Island body shop getting ready for Stirling Moss tomorrow. (It was smashed up in a melee yesterday.) Then, John Edgar kindly offered me a 3.5 Ferrari, but it was not back together in time either. Then Austin Conley offered me his Porsche Spyder. I drove some practice laps in it during the morning and loved it, but that was the car that broke an oil line. So I was rideless again. Then Carl Haas, of Lincolnwood, Ill., bravely lent me his black Porsche Spyder and so off I went in a strange car.
>
> It worked out fine, though, because Marian (sic) Lowe, who drove (Lou) Brero's D-Jaguar, lost a whole lap somewhere and Sammie (sic) Chapin, of Grosse Pointe, Mich., driving Boynton's two-litre Ferrari, spun several times. So, I won.
>
> But in the second race, I was again without a ride because Haas had only enough tires for the big

race tomorrow. Kimberly, president of Sports Car Club of America, trundled out his lovely little red O.S.C.A., showed me how to start it and there I was again driving a stranger. I led as far as the first sharp turn and then began the first of several goofs. By the time I recovered from that spin and got started again, there was no one in sight.

They tell me it was [a] close race between Mrs. Lowe [D-Jaguar] and Sammie [Ferrari]. Mrs. Lowe won. I only spun the O.S.C.A. once more so I was fifth behind Evelyn Mull, of Malvern, Pa., in her AC Bristol and Suzy Dietrich, of Sandusky, Ohio, in a Porsche Spyder. That gave Sammie the Ladies' Cup on well deserved points, and Evelyn, Suzy and I tied for second.

The second heat was, in fact, run at a blistering pace, so much so that winner Marion Lowe's first comment upon pulling her Jag to a halt was, "Women aren't supposed to drive that fast."

A wonderful ten-minute black-and-white Pathé newsreel of the races spotlights Moss's runaway victory over Gregory and de Portago for the Nassau Trophy in Bill Lloyd's Maserati 300 S, but also includes plenty of local color and an extended look at the women's events. The latter coverage shows Mull good-naturedly accepting assistance after a mishap and McCluggage pulling off her helmet, joyously astonished upon knowing she'd won the first. What both the film and McCluggage missed was what slowed Mull on the second run, a loose fastener that allowed the bonnet lid of her A.C.-Bristol to distractingly, even dangerously flap up and down.

The mood was buoyant and untroubled, the surroundings exciting or soothing as you wished, the mix of people and cars stupendous. For anyone looking to put a finger on the essence of 1950s sports car competition— the buzz over cars, the social energy, the fluid informality, the intensity of concentration when the time came—the Bahamas Speed Week in 1956 (and again in 1957) is the place to find it.

THE GREATEST YEAR

*I'll drive your car, I'll do my best to win for you, but
I'm not gonna fuck you.*

—RUTH LEVY TO JOHN EDGAR

A year in which motor racing rose to its greatest
heights in activity and public interest." So it
seemed then to the *New York Times*, and so it
does now. Everything that had been happening in sports
car racing—the development of the cars, the maturity of
the drivers, its popularity with fans, the opening of new
venues, the dawning of awareness that great American
drivers ought to be able to make money doing what they
did best, and, yes, breakthroughs in the achievements of
the leading women drivers—all came together in the extraordinary year of 1957. The only difference between
the perspectives of then and now is that, at the time, the
banner year seemed like one more step forward into an

234

ever more glorious future. Fifty years later, it represents, in the words of the song lyric that for many evoked the Kennedy era, that one, brief shining moment before everything started fraying, fragmenting, and commercializing.

There was action everywhere—East Coast, West Coast, seven new courses inaugurated in the United States; great drivers like Moss, Hawthorn, Collins, and others tearing up the world's tracks, while Fangio won his greatest race at Nurburgring on his way to his fifth world championship; Hill and, soon, Shelby and Gregory heading to Europe where they would impress; fifteen year-old Mexican sensation Ricardo Rodríguez crashing the party; membership in the Sports Car Club of America surpassing 9000, and 1200 in the Cal Club. For American women it was a year when Levy, Mull, and McCluggage scored thrilling victories. In California it was also a season in which Parravano departed the scene and the von Neumann team broke up due to divorce, leaving the field wide open for John Edgar, in what he couldn't know would be his last championship season.

In the American sports racing world, the sport's growing success—attendance had boomed in 1956, and the new tracks opening up promised further gains—inevitably led to entrants and drivers feeling they ought to share a piece of the action. Prior to that, revenues generated by admission fees didn't amount to much more than what it cost the organizers to stage the events, with any modest excess added to the coffers of the club or association. In Europe, where significant races were normally staged under the auspices of the FIA, starting money was the norm, with cash prizes offered to the winners. Certainly, this seemed reasonable given all the time and work, not to mention risk, everyone put into competitive driving. But the most important word in the name Sports Car Club of America was still *Club*; its most influential board member and most successful entrant, Briggs Cunningham, came from the old gentlemen's school of sporting and he remained adamant about keeping racing on an amateur basis, as did the current president, Jim Kimberly.

In fact, the fault line had been visible since the beginning of the decade. Alec Ulmann, an aeronautical engineer by profession who was close to Automobile Racing Club of America founders Sam and Miles Collier and was involved in staging the 1948 Watkins Glen initial with them, hatched a scheme with his friends to put on an endurance race modeled on Le Mans at the former Hendricks Field, a World War II Air Force base in Central Florida where crews had trained to fly B-17s. Organized by Ulmann, his wife, Mary, and businessman friend Colonel C. D. Richardson, the initial Sebring event looked like the bastard hillbilly stepchild of Watkins Glen; there were no grandstands or public-address system, the pits were outfitted with folding card tables, and safety precautions consisted of a few bales of hay strewn alongside the course. The six-hour first running started at 3 P.M. on New Year's Eve 1950. When it was over, well after dark, the winners were Frits Koster and Bobby Deshon in a tiny Crosley Hot Shot. The victory was made possible by the fact that the race was run on the handicap system, a European tradition that allowed a much less powerful car like the Crosley, going at a much slower average speed, to beat the brawnier runner-up, Jim Kimberly's 2-liter Ferrari. The following year, Ulmann and the surviving Collier brother, Miles, ran for SCCA office on a ticket specifically challenging the amateur-only policy; Ulmann was eventually banished from the organization for his effrontery. He persisted with Sebring, upgrading the facilities, altering the track (although to this day part of it still traverses the old airfield), luring celebrated European drivers with starting money, winning AAA sanction in 1952 (when the SCCA deliberately upstaged it with a competitive event at Vero Beach a week earlier), and in 1953 linking with the FIA to make Sebring part of the Sports Car World Championship (the only other FIA-recognized American race was Indy). Just a list of the mid-1950s winners—Stirling

Moss/Bill Lloyd, Mike Hawthorn/Phil Walters, Juan Manuel Fangio/Eugenio Castellotti, Jean Behra/Fangio—provides an idea of how rapidly Sebring became the most significant international racing destination in the United States, and a place where American drivers could begin to compete with the world's greatest champions. In 1956, Sebring offered $10,000 in prize money, and the SCCA started bending its rules by allowing its members to compete as long as any winnings were donated to charity. The policy paid off, as Phil Hill teamed with Peter Collins to win in 1958 and Hill, Dan Gurney, and Chuck Daigh, along with Olivier Gendebien, took the checkered flag in 1959, when Sebring hosted the first Formula 1 race on American soil. The setting proved inhospitable to Formula 1 followers, however; the disappointing turnout prompted a move the following year to Riverside in California.

The SCCA and the smaller but influential Cal Club held their ground in the battle for sustained amateurism, but Sebring was not the only hole in the dike. Some rival entities began staging events, and Tony Parravano was banished for a year by the SCCA and the CSCC for participating in one of them. Ken Miles, a top driver and Cal Club official, was himself briefly banned by the SCCA over some irregularities. Perhaps worst of all, marquee-name drivers, led by Phil Hill but with Masten Gregory,

Carroll Shelby, Richie Ginther, and others not far behind, began following the green to Europe and elsewhere; American drivers were permitted to keep starting prize money overseas. It was ironic that, even for this short time, the world headquarters of capitalism proved so un-accommodating to the idea of athletes profiting from their abilities, although racing was far from the only sport to suffer from the amateur/professional conun-drum; tennis, golf, and, up until recently, Olympic sports have struggled with the same issues.

In Los Angeles in early January 1957, Ruth Levy was trying to figure out how to take her obviously talented game to the next level. She had turned all heads in Los Angeles, but wasn't sure how she'd move on from driving her own car. The answer came with the help of Bill Gardner, her in-the-know pal, who advised her to pay a visit to Willow Springs, fifty miles north of Los Angeles, on a particular day. She went, along with Dan Gurney and Skip Hudson, ostensibly to learn the new course. But who else should be there, as Gardner knew they would, but Carroll Shelby, whom Ruth had never met, and John Edgar. Shelby told Ruth that his patron was looking for a woman to add to his stable of drivers. Ruth had already provided sufficient proof on the track that she was worthy of a ride with Edgar. In one of her versions of the tale, Ruth won the official Edgar seal of approval for outrageousness by warning him that she would accept his offer "on one condition. I'll drive your car, I'll do my best to win for you, but I'm not gonna fuck you."

Practically overnight, on January 20, Ruth was behind the wheel of Edgar's Porsche 550 Spyder in soggy Pomona, watching in her mirror as she sprayed rainwater in the faces of her closest rivals, Mary Davis and Betty Shutes. The following month she had her first ominous encounter with a too-big car. At New Smyrna Beach, in Florida, the 550 was cracked up in practice by someone else, so Ruth was given Shelby's monstrous 4.9 Ferrari, a V-12. When she begged off, Shelby told her she'd have no problem: "Point it down the straight and make sure you get it all around the corner before you kick it." Propped up in the cockpit by pillows all around so she could see and reach the pedals, Ruth not only kicked it but flipped it, upside down into the sand. Carted off by ambulance, she was okay, and bounced back by winning six ladies' events in a row—including another showdown with Mary and Betty at Paramount Ranch in June and races in Palm Springs and Santa Barbara—and placing an impressive fifth overall at Stockton. Ruth was well on her way to racking up more national points with the SCCA than any other woman on the West Coast.

Ruth's automotive fling with John Edgar had a soft landing in June at Elkhart Lake's Road America, where flame-outs by two big cars Shelby was supposed to drive put the onus on Ruth to make the Edgar team's trip worthwhile. She managed a decent sixth, but the result convinced Edgar that his future did not rest with Porsches or Ferraris; he sold his stock of both to Phoenix businessman Stan Sugarman. Ruth and Jack McAfee from Edgar's team went along, but the riotous good times of the tight and congenial Edgar unit were abruptly a thing of the past.

For several months, Ruth Levy and Denise McCluggage had been hearing a lot about each other, and they finally met late that summer when they were teamed in the Road America 500 in Wisconsin. "We hit it off right away," says Ruth, and nearly every photograph of the two of them together testifies to great humor and complicity between them. Their first collaboration, however, became a bust when Denise's 550 RS sputtered to a stop a third of the way through the race with a leaky intake manifold. Their subsequent two encounters that year, however, would be anything but uneventful.

◻ ◻ ◻

In Connecticut, the new mile-and-a-half course at Lime Rock made a warm debut on a hot April 28, as 6,600 people arrayed themselves across green hillsides to witness nine ten-lap races. Bruce Kessler, now legal at twenty-one, came out from California with a Ferrari Testa Rossa and looked like he was going to win the main until being outgunned and out-turned by Walt Hansgen's D-Jag on the last lap. The other outstanding contest had come in the fourth, for two-liter production cars, in which Jordan King, in an A.C.-Bristol, maintained a ten-second lead through seven laps. But Evelyn Mull, in her own A.C., steadily closed the gap to where she was only one second behind heading into the final go-round, which is how it ended. King again nosed out Evelyn by a second at the Mount Equinox hill climb in June.

But July belonged to Evelyn. Still often described in the press in such genteel women's-pages terms as a "44-year-old blonde with the figure of a 20-year-old and the charm of a Philadelphia Main Line hostess," Evelyn, accompanied by husband John as always, set out for Lime Rock again to battle thirteen men in a Class D and E production car run on July 11. It proved to be the most hotly contested race of the day, a thriller in which five drivers covered twenty laps with barely a few feet separating them. But in the end it was Evelyn who prevailed in her Ace-Bristol. On July 28, the siren call of Lime Rock was heeded once again for the New England Regional Championships, and again Evelyn won in the Class E event, finishing sixth overall. Sandwiched in between these was another victory for Evelyn, in race three at Thompson.

During this momentous summer, Denise was racing whenever possible, although she still had to make her *Herald Tribune* deadlines every weekend. When her Porsche pooped out at Elkhart Lake, for instance, there was no time for commiseration; everyone marveled at her professionalism as she headed straight to her typewriter to begin writing up her coverage.

Among the men, the Eastern summer was dominated by Shelby driving Ferraris for Edgar and by Hansgen, who, driving Jaguar D-types for Briggs Cunningham with no Californians in sight, took Watkins Glen and the inaugural mains at Bridgehampton and Virginia International. Out West, it was the summer of Ken Miles' seven straight Porsche Spyder victories, and John von Neumann, his top competition gone or elsewhere, won race after California race, mostly in Ferrari Testa Rossas.

The big event on the calendar was the opening of Riverside International Raceway. Intended to become *the* racing venue in Southern California, it had been the brainchild of longtime Cal Club member Rudy Cleye, a backer of the Grand Prix restaurant, and was designed along classic European lines, with unusual turns, a difficult series of snaky "s's" and a distinctive overall layout meant to attract Formula 1 to the site. But once he'd bought the 640-acre plot out toward the desert sixty miles east of Los Angeles and cleared all the development hurdles, Cleye ran out of cash. John Edgar came to the rescue with an initial infusion of $100,000.

The opening event was staged by the Cal Club, and an impressive crowd of thirty thousand turned out over the weekend of September 21–22. Unfortunately, on the very first day, a driver named John Lawrence was killed when his MG flipped over. One of the first events was the ladies' race, which promised to be a doozy and was. With Josie von Neumann off for the year with marriage and pregnancy, it looked to be a battle once again between Ruth and Mary Davis in a series that had thus far tilted in the newcomer's favor. Ruth, in a Porsche 550, and Mary, in an Aston Martin, were at each other's throats all the way, running as even as two cars can right down to the finish line, which Ruth reached one tenth of a second sooner than Mary.

After Shelby cracked up in practice, John Edgar was gratified that his young driver Richie Ginther was able to step up to take the big event in a Ferrari 410, giving Edgar a glorious win at the new track he put on the map. But the real sensation of the first Riverside was Ricardo Rodríguez. Not even old enough for a driver's license in California, fifteen-year-old Ricardo, along with his brother

Pedro, two years older, had been indulged all his life by wealthy parents, including the purchase of pricey new European racing machines. Their rich industrialist father, Don Pedro, had been a trick motorcycle rider in his youth and introduced both his sons to that sport, and they both became champions in their early teens, one after the other. At fifteen, Pedro was sent to school in the United States and, in his absence, Ricardo's career skyrocketed. Only five feet two but handsomely confident, Ricardo became a national sensation, moving from bikes to cars and graduating from a Topolino Fiat to O.S.C.A.s and Porsches. In early 1957, Gus Vignolle, publisher of *Motorsport*, saw Ricardo in a Mexican race and plastered his West Coast magazine with raves about his discovery. Thus was the stage set for Ricardo's American debut. When he zoomed off with the 1500cc class race at Riverside, the local reaction was similarly breathless. Everyone noted the incredible smoothness and control of Ricardo's driving; Shelby and Ginther were there to witness it that day, and the word went out.

A once-in-a-lifetime opportunity presented itself in October. Denise McCluggage called Ruth Levy to ask if she'd like to co-drive Briggs Cunningham's Porsche 550 RS with her at the upcoming Venezuelan Grand Prix. Ruth's reaction was instantaneous and predictable, but was not without complications; for her fiancé, Chuck

Rosher, who already felt left out of all the exciting action in his intended bride's life, this was the last straw. Undoubtedly knowing the result, Chuckles put his foot down, telling Ruth that if she got on the plane, their relationship was over.

In New York, Ruth saw Denise's cozy Village apartment and two giant Siamese cats, whereupon they took off for Caracas. The extraordinary distinction they enjoyed, of being the first all-female American team entered in an international championship race, was overshadowed by the chaos that greeted them upon arrival: The crème de la crème of the racing world had been invited to participate in a major event in a capital experiencing a political uprising. The corrupt dictator Colonel Marcos Perez Jimenez, who had taken power in a military coup in 1952, was being challenged by discontented liberal junior officers, the beginning of a revolt that would force him to flee the following year. During the Grand Prix, Caracas was under virtual martial law. "Everywhere you turned there was a gun in your face," Ruth remembers. "We had soldiers in the hallways of the hotel and they were all over the track." At the same time, there were no curfews for the foreign visitors, who indulged in the usual excesses of libations and extended nightlife. "It was party-ville down there," Ruth enthused. "I had a blast!" Part of the reason was that she met Ulf Norinder, a rich Swede and aspiring driver, with whom it was lust at first sight. Two nights before the November 3 race, all the visiting drivers jammed into taxis to examine the course for the thousand-kilometer epic, which was laid out on the city's main highways in a way that resembled a narrow, elongated paper clip, a configuration Phil Hill likened to a "surrealist nightmare." They worrisomely noticed an unusual profusion of stone abutments, many of which crumbled or came loose during the race to contribute to the many accidents.

The race itself was mayhem. Every single Maserati on the road was wrecked, beginning with a mishap involving Masten Gregory on the second lap, prompting the marque to pull back from competitive racing and concentrate on production cars. Both Ruth and Denise have devastating memories of the well-liked French-born American driver Harry Schell, whose car was hit by an errant wheel from Jo Bonnier's Maser and exploded. Ruth, who had dated Bonnier, says, "I have a picture of Harry Schell, standing there in flames beside his burning car. We had to drive past that." Denise remembers "Harry in the pits, shirtless, his arms bandaged to above his elbows, ultra-violet with purple gelatin. His face was like a reverse raccoon with only the area his goggles had covered free of blackening soot. His wild eyes were staring yet into the fire in his mind." Schell survived the accident, but was killed in a crash during practice at Silverstone in England on a Friday the 13th three years later.

There was a weirdly distracting element to the Caracas race for the two Americans: Once the locals figured out which car the women were driving, they threw flowers into the Porsche every time they came around a particular slow corner. But Denise and Ruth not only survived the obstacle course, but did so impressively, with a fourth in class and thirteenth overall in a race finished by only nineteen cars. Phil Hill, with whom Denise had recently started a romantic entanglement that would last several years, succeeded in winning the race, teamed with Peter Collins in a Ferrari 335S.

Due to Caracas, Ruth missed the second Palm Springs National on the same weekend, and with it the chance to redeem her disappointing third-place finish the year before. But she was back in time for the fall's Riverside SCCA National on November 17 and checked off victories in both ladies' events in the trusty Edgar/Sugarman 550. The main event that day was one for the ages, and one that involved most of the leading players of a memorable year. Dominant drivers Shelby and Gregory, both in Ferrari 450Ss, and Hansgen, in a D-Jag, jockeyed for the lead, along with the hitherto little-known Dan Gurney in a Ferrari 375 Plus. Shelby spun out and was forced to overtake most of the field from way back, and he did so to win the race and cap an amazing personal season.

Finally at year's end came the showdown that had to take place sooner or later, races that would pit the best women in American racing against one another; not exactly Ali vs. Frazier, Palmer vs. Nicklaus, Connors vs. McEnroe, Moss vs. Fangio, but as good as it got at the time for women who drove fast cars. Naturally, Evelyn Mull—who would shortly be named Female Driver of the Year by the *New York Times* and had accumulated more SCCA points than any other woman on the circuit—would be there, as would perennial contenders Suzy Dietrich, Joan Speidel, and others. But everyone headed down to Nassau in early December 1957 knew the battle royal would be the one of East vs. West, Denise McCluggage against Ruth Levy.

Denise instigated it. In Caracas, she had become convinced she was faster than Ruth and decided to invite her two-time co-driver to be her guest in the Bahamas. Even in a sport of friendly rivalries, where competitors by day almost invariably dined and partied together at night, Denise's chumminess seemed unusual, given that in Nassau, your "guest" was meant to share a room with you. In her article "Ruth Levy, Me, Nassau," first published in *AutoWeek* in 1988 and reprinted in her wonderful anthology *By Brooks Too Broad for Leaping* in 1994,

Denise felt compelled to explain something of her attitude about competition.

"When it came to competition I have a strange advantage. I had a dual childhood. I played dress-up and poured sugary tea for assorted dolls and teddy bears. I went to birthday parties in puffed-sleeved dresses with a big bow smack in the middle of my head. But I also raised hell with cap guns, jumped off the garage roof with an umbrella and played tackle football with the boys. I had to 'rassle' a few of them who moved into the neighborhood bearing a notion that girls shouldn't be allowed to play real football, but once the point was made we were all friends in the huddle. What I'm saying is, I was used to being best friends with my best competitors. Something, I keep reading, that is still lacking in today's corporate woman. Well, there are benefits to having a *boyhood* whether you're male or female."

Denise amusingly demonstrated another bonus of her boisterous childhood during Speed Week that year. During an afternoon of playtime on the beach, Denise spotted a coconut shaped exactly like a football and rallied a group of young race drivers to a game. Once they'd chosen up sides, Denise, who reveled in tackle football as a youngster and liked it played *hard*, was lined up opposite her towering friend from Texas, Carroll Shelby. At the snap, Denise was off the line in the sand

and slammed with full force into Shelby. They both fell down, but Shelby got the worse of it, grabbing his shoulder and screwing up his face in pain. As Denise began apologizing, Shelby grumbled, "Hell, you're big enough to go bear huntin' with a switch anyway." Later that evening, Stirling Moss, scheduled to face Shelby for the Nassau Trophy two days later, told Denise, "I've got a list of other chaps I'd like you to play football with before the race." Taped up and numbed with painkiller—no one was sure if his shoulder was broken or dislocated—Shelby gave Moss a helluva time on the track, finishing the fifty-lap, 250-mile race in his Maserati 450S less than a second behind Moss's borrowed Ferrari 290MM, with Phil Hill in a Ferrari 335S just one second back of Shelby.

Moss wasn't supposed to be driving the Ferrari but was forced to do so because of what Ruth Levy did to his Aston Martin DBR2 in the mano a mano with Denise on the new Oakes Course at the former commercial airfield. The moment the ladies' races were over, Denise had to run back and file her account of it for her *Herald Tribune* readers on December 8:

> The ladies' race, a fifty-mile event run in two heats of twenty-five miles each (five laps), was said to be the most exciting of the meet so far. It seemed so from the seat of a Porsche 55 RS.

The second heat saw two of the women drivers crash but no serious injury results. Ruth Levy of Belair, Calif., had borrowed the 3.7 Aston Martin that was to be driven tomorrow by Stirling Moss, winner of the Nassau Trophy last year. She was a breath in second place (behind my Porsche) in the first heat. And on the last turn of the last lap of the second heat went deep into the hairpin in a last-ditch attempt to pass me. The car, bigger and heavier than she is used to, plowed off the road and flipped twice. She was thrown clear into the bushes that border the course and was scratched and bruised.

Suzy Dietrich, of Sandusky, Ohio, who had driven to a clean third place in her small 1,100 c.c. Elva during the first heat, went off the road in the first lap of the second heat on a sharp left corner known as Blackbeard's Corner and demolished her car. She, too, escaped serious injury.

My Porsche was thus first in both heats. Mrs. Mull, who did a smooth job finishing fourth the first time and third the second, was second overall. (Isabelle Haskell, of Red Bank, N.J., was second in the second heat in an O.S.C.A. However, the car was second running well and she missed most of the first heat.)

Third in the combined reckoning of the two heats of the ladies' race was Jean Speidel, of Miami, Fla., in a Porsche 55.

The account in the *Nassau Guardian*, which ran photographs of Ruth conferring before the race with both Denise and Stirling Moss, called the matchup "thrilling" and "a blistering duel," and was able to add only that Ruth, despite her protestatons that she wasn't hurt, was taken by ambulance to Princess Margaret Hospital, where she spent the night, and that Denise had averaged 96.292 miles per hour in the first heat and 95.298 in the second.

In her *AutoWeek* piece about the weekend written thirty years later, Denise oddly suggests that Ruth got the ride in the Aston Martin by using womanly wiles on a receptive Moss—oddly, that is, if it's not true. Ruth, hardly shy about confiding her various liaisons, categorically insists there was never anything between her and the British ace. To the contrary, she says, she didn't even want to get in the Aston Martin, much less race against Denise in it; it had no seat belt, they had to stuff a pillow behind her so she could reach the pedals, it "steered worse than a Ford truck" and, after what had happened to her before in big, hard-to-handle cars, as at New Smyrna Beach a few months earlier, she knew her limits. She tried to demur, but Moss talked her into it.

Ruth had been all set to challenge Denise in her favorite Spyder, but its engine had blown out when Sugarman loaned it to someone else for practice. With virtually
no time to get used to the Aston Martin, Ruth neverthe-
less did quite well with it in the first heat, pressing Denise
all the way. But there was something Ruth didn't realize
at the time, revealed by Denise in her piece. "I went too
wide in the first swooping turn and found myself skit-
tering along in marbles—small stones and tiny chunks of
asphalt. And I spun. But I think I'm the only one who
knows that. I completed a fast, lucky 360 and resumed the
chase. Before the first lap was done I was back in the
midst of it. I knew then I could win; it was just a matter
of picking the right place to pass so Ruth couldn't get me
back with the Aston's superior acceleration and out-drag
me to the finish line.

"And, too, it was a matter of staying out of Ruth's
way. Her West Coast reputation had a streak of wildness
and here she was, sending oil barrels flying."

Denise did what she needed to do to nip Ruth in the
first heat, but even though in the second she was leading by several car lengths heading toward the final turn
of the final lap, she was worried that unless she made a
particularly fine turn, the Aston might enable Ruth to
overtake her in the final hundred yards. As Denise went

into the two-part hairpin, Ruth "just kept coming, getting larger in my mirror as I was setting up for the turn. There in the mirror the green Aston growing bigger and greener. Already I was beyond my cut-off point and she kept coming on the inside—*accelerating*, not braking. I wasn't about to turn in front of her, she'd collect me as a hood ornament.

"So I held my straight line deep into the turn, braking to a near stop. And *whoosh!* Ruth whipped by me, straight off the end of the pavement and disappeared into the brush. I scrambled around the turn, took the checker and then dashed back to the place where Ruth had put a large dark hole into the underbrush."

In Ruth's account, she was confident she could beat Denise as she made her rapid gains going into the hairpin. "I took it sideways, just to punch it to go into the straightaway—the plan was to drift through the corner. You could have towed the car through the corner and still beat her. But I hit a piece of coral with the rear right wheel, I hit it and went straight up in the air. I went out of the car like this"—she leans back in a spread-eagle—"and I remember screaming, and while in the air I remember I felt I was in someone's gentle hands, then *boom!* I swear I saw the white light. I saw lots of people. Then I felt hands, with pieces of white coral on either side."

All Ruth needed at the hospital were a few stitches in an elbow, and she remembers Stirling Moss coming to visit her that evening. Someone, maybe Moss, asked Ruth if she'd run out of brakes in the turn. "No," she said, "I ran out of brains."

Running On Fumes

You couldn't just show up with a car and race anymore.

—Mary Davis

Ruth Levy drove back to Los Angeles with her Swedish boyfriend Ulf Norinder in his trendy Mercedes Gullwing. "I hated it," she says of the car, which just added to her grumpiness over the Nassau debacle. Her mood told her this racing thing was all over before she knew it was over. Ruth hadn't been badly injured when she was tossed out of the Aston Martin, but she was seriously unnerved. As with bullfighters who have been gored, drivers often get skittish or lose their confidence after a crash, and Ruth had now endured two accidents where she lost control of a car that she could tell in advance might be too much for her.

Some competitors bounce back from such doubts—others don't, and Ruth never really did.

In early 1958, Ruth took up her usual schedule of races, beginning with the sixth Pomona meet on February 8, a day that ranks as one of the venue's best, and the ladies' race was one of the reasons why. Ruth was grateful simply to get behind the wheel of a Porsche again, an RS, a faster car than the 550 of her chief rival in the race, Betty Shutes. As the *West Coast Sports Car Journal* wrote of the Pomona run:

> No one expected anything but a Levy levee, but Betty Shutes was to put her in Porsche worth. Ruth, in a borrowed car, dropped the lever into third, apparently, instead of first at the start and was considerably behind when Betty shot into the lead. With determination and skill she overhauled Miss Shutes but Betty wasn't having any. She kept Ruth hanging for the six laps, winning by a mere .01 sec. Barbara Windhorst did extremely well to keep her Morgan within 10 seconds of the dueling Spyders for third.

Ruth admits she made the mistake of starting in third gear in the race, "a rare instance of driver error!"

Ruth agreed to team up with Denise again, this time

in the 12 Hours of Sebring endurance run in March. It was "a fun little ride," she says, but was also a bit demoralizing as, from the seat of their distinctly uncompetitive little 747cc Fiat-Abarth, they could only watch Stirling and Phil and all the rest zoom past them during the race and wave. Soon after, there was an event at Paramount Ranch—one of her two favorite courses, Elkhart Lake being the other—where she wasn't even able to get a ride. "I didn't say good-bye to anybody, I walked out and I left. That was it, then and there." A while later, she took her daughter Pam to watch a race at Riverside. "It had all changed. The corporate stuff was everywhere. A voice from the stands yelled, 'Are you Ruth Levy?' and I said, 'I wish,' and I left. It was the last race I ever saw."

In the opinion of her fond rival Denise McCluggage, "Ruth lost it" after the Nassau accident, something she felt when she drove with Ruth again in Florida. "Ruth is an extremely talented person, a terrifically interesting person," Denise enthuses. "She can sing great blues and jazz, writes poetry—she paints. Racing was just part of that. It was something she got attention for. She needed that kind of excitement. She liked getting attention from men, and she got it. She was so vibrant. I think she's a terrific girl. She's a gutsy girl, boy."

With Ruth abruptly out of the picture, the way was clear for Josie von Neumann to virtually run the table in

California ladies' races. Josie returned in the summer of 1958 after a year and a half off, during which time she had married John McLaughlin, who had worked for her stepfather and also dated Ruth Levy, and had her only child, a son, James. Driving a 250 Testa Rossa, she aced the rest of the female field in a slew of races, in August finishing first at Nevada's Minden Racetrack as well as at Santa Barbara, winning both the ladies' and the main at Del Mar on September 21, taking the ladies' and third in the main at San Diego's Hourglass Field one week later, and prevailing once more in the ladies' race at Laguna Seca in November.

Finally achieving her goal of racing in major events against men rather than in ladies' races, Josie performed more than respectably in 1959 racing the 250 TR under the banner of her mother Eleanor, who took over the von Neumann stable of cars in her pricey divorce settlement with John. She took a seventh at Pomona in February, a fourth at Mexico's Avandero course in April, a third in a Mexico City contest in May, fourth at Hourglass in June and sixteenth at Vaca Valley in September. However, the big ones were at Riverside. On July 19, the von Neumann name was done proud by Richie Ginther, Eleanor's long-ago mechanic, who won the tough 150-mile Grand Prix in a Ferrari 412 MI, and by Josie, who in the same race ran fourteenth overall out of eighteen finishers; thirty-three drivers had started. At the heavily ballyhooed October 11 Riverside Times Grand Prix, won by Phil Hill in a 250 TR59, Josie made her final significant statement in a race with an eleventh-place overall finish. Now twenty-seven, Josie could still drive well, but with nearly eight years of racing behind her was willing to admit, "I can't go as fast as the men, and I am aware of my own shortcomings." Foremost among these was the difficulty of concentration during an extended race. "You have to have nerves of ice and ignore the other drivers so that they don't pressure you. That's the hardest thing there is for me." With this, she slipped away from the scene, raised her son, listened to her beloved jazz and blues records and surrounded herself with countless cats at her new home in Ojai. She developed diabetes and passed away, at sixty-five, in 1997.

Thinning the competition further were the phase-outs of Mary Davis and Ginny Sims, who together moved into a distinctly different automotive arena. The Mobilgas Economy Run was designed to test the fuel economy of new cars under real road conditions to suggest to average everyday drivers what kind of mileage they might expect to get. Launched in 1936 by Gilmore Gasoline as a one-day trip from Los Angeles to Yosemite and continued and expanded by Mobil after it bought the small independent company, the heavily publicized annual spring run involved cars in eight competitive classes, chosen off showroom floors at random, which were then driven 2500 miles—exclusively in second gear—to break them in. As to the driving, it was similar to running rallies, in that the object was not speed but driving properly in a manner meant to maximize the car's gas mileage, and by not cheating in ways that ordinary drivers wouldn't know about. Every car had a driver and "co-driver," who was more of a navigator and technique advisor and didn't actually get behind the wheel. Riding as passengers in the backseat were two Auto Club observers who kept close tabs on mileage and any possible infractions, for which the drivers would be penalized.

Women had never been accepted as drivers in the Economy Run, but when the restriction was lifted in 1957, the public relations guys at Plymouth made a beeline for the movie-star-dazzling Mary Davis to drive their car. Initially, Carol Givens was to join her as co-driver on the four-day journey in April, but for varying reasons—Carol claimed a job conflict while Mary said she still felt raw over Carol's financial betrayal at the Grand Prix—Carol was replaced by Ginny Sims. During the break-in period, they learned to manage their Belvedere V-8 well, keeping to about forty-five miles per hour, not pressing on the inclines and hills, driving smoothly, "like there was an egg behind the gas pedal," Mary noted. All the Auto Club observers seemed to be from the California Institute of Technology, earnest young men with shirt-pocket penholders in place and clipboards in hand, and obstinately humorless, hardly the types these women were accustomed to. "Oh, the guys were nerds!" whoops Mary, who tried little tricks to better mileage like driving on the shoulder. But she couldn't slip anything past the onboard "police," as the women teasingly called the scrupulous meter readers.

Much to the delight of Plymouth and its driving team, Mary and Ginny won in the Class A low-price field, averaging 21.3907 miles per gallon on the 1568-mile run from Los Angeles to Sun Valley, Idaho, April 14–18. As Mary had been the driver and Ginny had to return to her film-lab job, Mary got the lion's share of attention. "Strangely enough," Mary points out, "despite all my racing activities, it was driving a car slowly that brought me to the attention of the media." Touted as "The World's Greatest Woman Driver" from coast to coast, she appeared frequently on television and made personal appearances everywhere; her glamorous, busty blond looks represented the ideal of the time, and she reaped the rewards, becoming far more famous for winning the Economy Run than for any race she ever ran. "We got paid a nominal amount to drive it, but I got checks for years for the commercials from Chrysler, and got mink stoles for going to car dealers," says Mary, who noted one other side benefit: "The macho set started to treat me with a bit more respect." Mary continued the Economy Runs with her best friend for four more years, always from Los Angeles to different annual destinations, such as Kansas City, Minneapolis, and Chicago. After 1961, Mary was too involved with her real-estate projects to continue, but Ginny persisted until 1968, when, on the fifth night of that year's run, Martin Luther King was shot. The event was immediately canceled and never resumed. Ginny ended up in Indianapolis and got a big thrill driving her Ford around the fabled brickyard, even though she couldn't even crack one hundred miles per hour. But then Ginny was taken out in a real Indy car by Danny Oaks. "That got my heart started," she enthuses.

One other Southern California driver who stayed with the Economy Run to the bitter end was long-ago Cal Club secretary and organizer Mary O'Connor. Although she never raced, Mary was drawn to the slow precision of the driving demanded by this event. Participating the first time as navigator to Ruth Doushkess, she drove thereafter and won her class in a Chevy in 1963. Unlike Mary Davis, however, she shunned the limelight her victory could have provided her. "Mary Davis and I are best friends, but we're totally the opposite. She loves all the publicity—bring on the cameras and the lights and the attention!—but I'm just really Indiana, happy to stay in the background. I'm more of a voyeur."

Intertwined emotional and business reasons pushed Mary Davis out of sports car racing. When giving Bob Drake some involvement and an income at the Grand Prix didn't get him out of her hair, Mary finally had to do what she simply hadn't been strong enough to do before: cut herself off from her husband. "Nobody knows what the fear of a person is like unless you're in it," Mary says. A master manipulator, Drake alternately threatened her, told her he'd never let her leave, and ridiculed her for even imagining she could. When Mary finally summoned up the nerve to tell him she wanted a divorce, all Drake said was, "Why? I'm fine the way I am." No matter what she said, Drake always had some kind of cockamamie, self-centered counter to it, and she finally promised him half her income if he'd give her a divorce. He agreed, but then said, "'How do I know you'll keep your offer?' Can you imagine, after all those years . . ." Mary ended up giving Drake the Grand Prix as well as her cherished Mercedes 300SL. But what really mattered to her was the oceanfront property she borrowed one million dollars to buy down the coast in Redondo Beach. Recounting it to Bill Pollack years ago as if in a scene straight out of a movie, Mary recalled how she took her working-class mother to the vacant property and said,

"'Mom, I'm going to build a hotel right there, and a marina. I'm gonna do it. By myself.' And she simply couldn't believe it. No one in our family had ever made out so well."

Mary's original partner in what became the Portofino Inn in Redondo Beach was Frank Arciero, a well-known Southern California construction magnate who had launched his own racing team in 1957. Frank's life story was dramatically similar to that of Tony Parravano: the journey from rural Italian poverty to Detroit, a well-timed postwar move to Southern California, immediate success in the concrete business and then construction, fast cars, and in Frank's case, celebrity as the godfather of the Indy Car-oriented Championship Auto Racing Teams and proprietor of a large Central California winery. But before construction was completed, the two had a falling out over money. According to Mary, Frank offered a low-ball figure to buy her out, whereupon she called upon secret resources to buy him out. Her aces were two gentlemen friends of means, William Keck of Imperial Oil in Southern California and Angelo Campadonico, a Schweppes dealer for the seven western states who lived in Northern California but would come down to see Mary every Monday. Evidently, each man knew nothing about the other, but Mary called upon them both and they obliged, which allowed her dream to come true.

Mary first put in the boat slips and opened the marina in 1962. The Portofino Inn had its grand opening in January 1964 and was an instant success. Encompassing the upscale hotel, two restaurants, an apartment building, some offices, and about one quarter of the yacht harbor slips, the Portofino immediately became *the* hangout for the racing crowd, not only for the Southern California gang but for drivers from all around the world when they were in town. The Indy guys—Mario Andretti, the Unsers, Peter Revson, Donohue—always stayed there, and so did the international crew Mary knew from the Grand Prix. The place earned further cachet when Brock Yates decided to make the Portofino the West Coast destination for his illegal cross-country Cannonball Run starting in 1971, and got another boost when it appeared in the all-star, Rat-Packy 1981 movie about the by-then-disbanded race. There was just one person not pleased with the motion picture's involvement. "My mother's name was Sammy Smith. But when the *Cannonball Run* crew came to the Portofino, they called my mother Sammy Davis and she got so mad!" At its peak, the inn achieved the third-highest annual occupancy rate—98 percent—of all hotels in the United States.

Technically, Mary had to quit racing for good because no one would insure her for the Portofino if she didn't. "But Bob ruined racing for me," Mary admits. "It wasn't fun for me to go to the track and see all his girlfriends around. At the same time, all the big shots came out with all their money and all their cars. It got to be too big. You couldn't just show up with a car and race anymore. The camaraderie was gone. Of course, I went on to better things with the Portofino."

Along the way, Mary became president of the Redondo Beach Chamber of Commerce and in 1981 she opened her own bank, the Bay Cities National Bank, which later merged with another one to her benefit. She was even approached to run for mayor, an offer she declined. In 1987, Mary cashed out handsomely, selling the Portofino for $15 million. She also dared, twenty-five years after ridding herself of Bob Drake, to marry again. The way she looked and as successful as she was, men hit on Mary every day. But due to her history with Drake, her guard was always up and she never let anyone get too close. Her solution, then, was to marry a buddy, someone she'd known for many years whom she knew she could trust. Steve Weidinger had been a bailiff at the local court and, due to his strong connections at city hall and with the city police, had helped Mary through considerable red tape during the construction of the Portofino. Finally splitting from his wife, Steve decided he'd like nothing better than to tend bar at the popular new watering hole, and Mary was happy to oblige. But the new gig didn't help his drinking problem, which may have hastened his demise. Mary bought a boat, intending to sail the world when and where she and her husband pleased, but the retirement dream didn't work out, as Steve died of cancer just four months after the wedding. Bob Drake died of brain cancer in 1990. Mary has lived comfortably at the beach and in the desert at La Quinta ever since.

Ginny Sims had gotten started racing later than Mary and most of the others, in 1956, and kept going a bit longer as well. Ginny loved racing for the pure fun of it, for giving dimension to her life. For five years, from 1957 through 1961, during which she raced at least once a month and drove the Mobilgas Economy Run every spring, "Life was beautiful and full, what with working in the studios and cutting film for a living." After a couple of years on the circuit, Ginny realized she was no longer a novice, even if she never felt as madly competitive as Ruth or Mary. In sports car racing, she maintains, "You don't want to kill yourself. You're doing it for fun. Nobody's paying you to go out there." Her professed career highlight came in 1959, when she won the fastest woman of the year trophy at Riverside Raceway for doing 163.4 miles per hour down the one-mile back straightaway in Art Evans' Devin SS, a time she claims was only two or three-tenths of a second over the men's record set by Richie Ginther. Riverside was always her favorite course: "All the turns and the straightaway, just the way it was set up was great."

By the late 1950s, Ginny had moved from General Film Lab on Selma to Paramount, where the head negative cutter, an old Irish gent named Pat O'Donnell, became both her surrogate father and boss, hiring her to cut negatives on the TV series *Bonanza* and *High Chapparral*. She went to Disney for a while, but when Pat retired she returned to Paramount in his old job. She remained on the track as long as she could, mostly racing Corvettes toward the end, often for Bob Bondurant, always ladies races only. Finally, she could see, "It was just over for us. The big people came in and we little people were out. The big timers got into road racing. In 1961 I had my last race, in a Corvette in Pomona, and that's all she wrote."

Ginny retired from Universal, where she had worked for the final eleven years of her film cutting career, in 1983. Twenty-three years later, at eighty-five, she looked about seventy-two, still stood five feet ten, didn't dye her still darkish hair and continued to travel the world, often with her still-best friend, Mary Davis, and sometimes on her own. Her one sorrow is her daughter Fran, who spent weekends with her mother at the tracks as a teenager, thought she would become a successful film and television actress in her twenties and didn't make it; she fell out with her mother and is, at last report, homeless and out of contact with her mother. Ginny says there is nothing she can do about it.

As for racing, though, "I was doing something that I loved and it gave me a better high than having a drink. It was the greatest thrill. You were really high. Getting that trophy in Riverside, that was a high. I still love speed."

Although the personal circumstances differed, it was more or less the same story with all the women; the circuit was changing too much, and there simply didn't seem to be a place for them anymore. Well into 1959, Linda Scott kept roaring through races in Otto Zipper's Talbot in fine style, although he switched cars on her at the last minute at the Memorial Day Santa Barbara Cal Club Regional and put her in a Porsche RS Spyder. The car stalled out at the start, but Linda finally got it going and amazed everyone by moving from dead last to challenge Betty Shutes for first place. (This was also the weekend Steve McQueen turned up to win the novice race.) It was a good way to go out. Linda had hoped to run in the October Riverside Times Grand Prix, the final major California race of the 1950s, which gave Josie one of her final triumphs. But Linda was five months pregnant with her second child, Teresa—she had earlier had a son, Chris—and she walked off the stage for good.

In the early 1960s, Linda divorced, married again, and shifted her interests from land to sea, building and crewing ocean-racing catamarans. With the end of that marriage came another change of environment and type of conveyance. With some time out to earn a degree in microbiology at the California Polytechnic Institute, Linda spent the better part of a decade as a bush pilot in Idaho and then Alaska. She then embraced an even more solitary existence on the fringe of the Mojave Desert near Edwards Air Force Base, working charter flights and flight instruction for Barnes Aviation. For the past decade, she's worked in what is called air attack for the Forest Service, directing the planes that help put out forest fires; Linda circles around in a Cessna Skymaster above the tanker planes, radioing them information about where to dump next.

Evelyn Mull was on a roll heading into 1958. Being named the *New York Times* Woman Sports Car Driver of the Year for 1957 brought her heavy publicity and a round of cocktails, functions, and appearances over the holidays; there were many interviews and, as usual, lots of pictures of her in the papers. Appearing at a gymkhana in Bergen, New Jersey, she was asked the usual questions about her husband's support for her driving, and she said, "My husband is marvelous! He always gives me the better car. He loves to race, regardless of where he finishes." She added

that men had never given her a hard time about competing with them and that, for her, the sex difference was a
non-issue, because "you can't tell the difference when
you're wearing coveralls and a crash helmet."

It was Evelyn who gave the men a hard time later in
the year. On September 28, Evelyn became the first
woman to win a major race in the history of Watkins Glen,
beating twenty-four men in the third race, an eleven-lap
contest for D and E production and Class H modified
cars. From seventeenth position on the starting grid, she
pushed her A.C.-Bristol to first place within two laps. She
gave up the lead in the third and fourth laps, but pulled
back in front in the fifth to stay, beating second-place fin-
isher Archie Means, also in an Ace-Bristol, with a time in
the 25.3-mile race of 20:44:46.

The year also saw the publication of Evelyn's unique
little book, *Women in Sports Car Competition.* A brief
thing of 105 pamphlet-sized pages and put out by Sports
Car Press, the book is part useful who/what/where/how
primer about sports car racing at the time and part personal history of her own involvement in the sport with her
husband, with snapshot portraits of many of the women
who traveled in Evelyn's weekend racers circle. Asking a
few of her friends why they got into racing, Evelyn received a good, upper-class answer from Nancy Bailey, who
said, "I started in sailboats years ago, but they didn't go

fast enough. I was introduced to sports cars—they did. I highly recommend sports-car racing to all young mothers who get slightly bored (as who doesn't) with the usual run of babies and housekeeping. Racing people are marvelous, wonderful, and you get lots of fresh air and sun—also grease, and gas fumes—but delightful." Pinkie Windridge said, "After a summer of going from race to race with Fred, I decided to give up my nine show horses and join him. He is all for it up to the point when I ask for a cute little RS like Denise's or a sweet little O.S.C.A. like Isabelle's."

Evelyn tracked down Josie von Neumann during her sabbatical and Josie told her she had stopped racing because "I found it very difficult to care for twenty cats, two dogs, two sheep, seven bunnies, two ducks, ten old Cadillacs, two MGs, a Rolls Royce, a pickup truck, a business, a house, and last but not least, a husband, and be able to take off for the weekend."

The breezy, informative tome provides a personal tour of the main racing venues. Evelyn's favorites: Lime Rock—"You can pile into the curves three and four cars abreast; at other places two cars at a time is plenty"; Thompson—"The track at Thompson starts on a slightly downhill grade, then swoops into a left turn, a sharp right, an upgrade, sharp left, uphill and a sharp right— you get the idea, never a monotonous moment,"; Bridge-hampton—"It is beautiful, and so fast that steps have

been taken to increase the margin of safety at all points";
and Road America at Elkhart Lake—"It's a beautiful and
interesting raceway, and its 'brats' sausages are superb!"

The book concludes with brief discourses on rallies, hill
climbs, and early racing history, and emphasizes how rapidly membership in the SCCA had grown in recent years
and how many women had come into the sport, with admittedly varying degrees of seriousness and ability. She
ends her unique survey with: "By the time this book is in
print the number of licensed women race drivers will
probably have increased by a third. And I know that if the
Sports Car races continue on their amateur basis, they will
find it as much fun as I have." This was written, and read,
in an upbeat spirit of open-ended promise for the sport, for
nowhere in the book do the threatening clouds of loom-
ing professionalism appear. In retrospect, however, the
crucial "if" of the final sentence represents Evelyn's tacit
acknowledgment that the future of "pure" sports car racing was uncertain, that things would likely not remain as
they were.

❐ ❐ ❐

The difference between amateur and professional auto
racing is clear from merely a glance at any photograph
of a 1950s SCCA or Cal Club race compared to one taken

at any non-club event after about 1959. In the former, the surroundings are pristine, even beautiful; spectators are scattered around wherever they like; cars are marked with only their numbers, and drivers wear either their own clothes or coveralls. In the latter, the tracks are securely fenced, fans are mostly confined to grandstands heavily festooned with advertisements, and everything that moves—drivers, team crews and automobiles—is branded as extensively as space permits. The difference defines in simple terms the two prevailing mindsets— that of the old-school purists who resisted change and capitulation, and that which recognized and embraced the unstoppable commercial forces that would engulf all sports, no matter how hitherto unsullied, in the coming decades. What began in the realm of fun and high-minded "sporting" competition ended up, within fifteen years, in the domain of marketing. There was no other way it could have gone.

In the world of sports car racing, the fissures were there for all to see for a number of years, ever since Sebring went its own way, however tentatively at first, and then with the assorted upstart race organizers at mid-decade. In a column in the January 1958 issue of *West Coast Sports Car Journal*, an organ of the Cal Club, Ken Miles clearly articulated the traditionalist position: "Sports car racing, on an amateur level, was and is essentially a participants' sport. The public is encouraged to attend the races and considerable concessions are made to provide an attractive spectacle, but essentially the races are staged by the club members for the club members, the object in view being to offer the drivers the best possible racing, yet be as fair as possible to every class of competition." He pointed out that, as the competition had grown more intense, "inevitably the group of serious competitors has formed a smaller and smaller percentage of the total membership, growing at a much slower rate than the membership at large."

In a purposely unspecific manner, Miles also laid into the rival SCCA for its "present refusal to allow drivers who they feel are not socially or politically acceptable to compete in their races." This was an allusion to an unpleasant instance of racial discrimination that was revealed in the March issue of the *Journal*. John Cooper, a very popular "colored" pianist at the El Matador club in San Francisco, Nob Hill resident, Austin-Healey driver, and member of nine foreign car clubs in the Bay Area, was sponsored for SCCA membership by the required two members, only to be rejected by a regional executive by the name of James Orr, since retired; although not stated as such, the use of the term "national precedent" suggested that Cooper was the first black candidate to be submitted for club membership. A huge protest ensued at the next board meeting, with the result that Cooper could reapply with the backing of two new sponsors and be rubber-stamped for membership by the new regional executive.

The factors adversely pressuring the amateur/club racing setup were numerous and weighty: The steady rise of Formula 1 and the allure of prize money and international recognition, which took top drivers from the sports car circuit—most notably Phil Hill, Carroll Shelby, Masten Gregory, and Richie Ginther—overseas; the crash and burn of all three of the top California entrants, first Tony Parravano, and then John von Neumann and John Edgar simultaneously; the quick rise and fall of Lance Reventlow's Scarab, which for a moment supercharged the Southern California racing environment but then collapsed when the car sputtered in the Grand Prix arena; the advent in 1958 of the United States Automobile Club's sports car division, which itself never amounted to much and was dissolved within four years but which forced the SCCA and Cal Club to open up, and, perhaps most of all, the pressure from within, from board members and drivers who began opening their eyes to what was going on around them and realized they had to move with the times or become irrelevant.

When the end came, it was with extraordinary suddenness. As Lynch, Edgar, and Parravano aptly put it in

"Sports Car Racing in the 1950s," the "Berlin Wall of amateurism" fell on October 12, 1958, when the first United States Grand Prix for sports cars was held at Riverside International Speedway. The large turnout for Southern California's next pro race, the FIA-sanctioned Pomona gathering on February 1, 1959, featuring numerous foreign drivers lured by the $15,000 prize money, further signaled that there was no going back. From that point on, it became much more difficult for venues to attract big crowds for race lineups which, without prize money or sponsors, featured second-string drivers in smaller cars that quickly began looking like vintage vehicles. As a result, to stay competitive, previously amateur-only courses started searching for sponsors, while on both sides of the country purists interested in fun and no profit began running in "private" races, where, to eliminate the growing expense of insurance, the public was not allowed. In line with Ken Miles' analysis of the growing split between "serious competitors" and driving-for-driving's-sake members, this practice prefigured the SCCA's eventual separation of events into "professional" and "club" status.

Of all the theories about why the bottom fell out of sports car racing as dramatically as it did, especially in Southern California, the most original one belongs to Mary O'Connor. She blames it entirely on the arrival of the baseball Dodgers, who moved from Brooklyn to Los Angeles in 1957 and, she insists, became the new focus of everyone's leisure time.

At the Cal Club, the erosion from the ranks of its leading entrants and drivers took a heavy toll, as did the transformation of several of its main venues into professionally oriented arenas. As in the East, a hard core of veterans objected to any change of status, but in 1961 the Cal Club was absorbed into the SCCA. Even stubborn holdouts like Bill Pollack finally came around. "At the time I was opposed to the Cal Club losing its independence, but in the end," he admits, "it definitely worked out for the best."

Specifically for the women, however, things did not work out for the best. For those who persisted, they raced when and where they could. In the East, Suzy Dietrich persevered—partly thanks to the busy driving schedule of her husband, Chuck—and continued to spice up her thirty-one-year tenure as a Sandusky, Ohio, librarian by racing at a high level into the late 1960s. Sometimes competing in big races with Chuck—he ran second in the 1963 Virginia International Raceway National Cup race on April 28, 1963, while she finished thirteenth out of a twenty-five-car field—Dietrich capped her career with a series of teamings with other women (notably the "Think Pink" bombshell Donna Mae Mims) in long-distance events like the 12 Hours of Sebring and the 24 Hours of Daytona. At the 1966 Daytona, Dietrich and Mims co-drove a Sunbeam Tiger—"the slowest car there," Dietrich remembers—with Janet Guthrie, although Dietrich recalls Mims saying of the future five-time Indy driver that, "I don't think we should let her in the car." The next year, Dietrich and Mims paired up in an ASA 411, finishing twenty-fourth at Daytona and twenty-fifth at Sebring in a race that saw Denise McCluggage and Marianne Rollo taking seventeenth. "The main thing in races like those," Dietrich says, "was to stay awake. You had to race for three hours at a time."

Mims is quite a story unto herself, although, having begun racing in 1961, she doesn't belong to the 1950s sports car generation. She was a Corvette girl from the Pittsburgh area—her business card elegantly announces her as "Fancier of Corvettes"—and she drew automatic attention to herself and won lots of fans with her pink cars, pink coveralls and crash helmet, and pink hair, a dye-job as well as a wig. Her friend Denise McCluggage feels that, "Driving to her was more of a self-promotional thing; the dizzy act, the pink Corvette. She was more what men expected women racers to be." Mims denies it. "People always ask me if all this pink talk is a gag or a publicity stunt. Absolutely not. I just happen to like pink—I feel pink. It's a girl color and I'm a girl."

Cutting through the argument is the fact that Mims was a pretty good driver, good enough to take the Cumberland B production national race in 1961 in her 1957 fuel-injected 'Vette, and two years later, in a Bugeye Sprite, to win a national championship, the SCCA title in Class H, a category with three hundred racing members in it. She was chased by sponsors thereafter, which is what got her the Daytona and Sebring rides, among others. She raced anywhere and in everything, including the Cannonball Run in a Cadillac limo with a bra company as a sponsor, before retiring in 1974. Back in the 1960s, like McCluggage, she worked at *Competition Press*, among other publications, as an auto-racing journalist.

Evelyn Mull might have continued racing longer than she did, save for the fact that her husband John had a bad accident in 1958 at Lime Rock—he flipped his Jag with his arm sticking out the side and was caught under it, breaking his hand—that brought his racing days to an end, and hers in the bargain; they had started racing together on the same day and would conclude the same way. It took John a year to recover, and thereafter the Mulls avidly returned to rallying. At this, Evelyn was a mountain master. Her daughter Nonny says, "She'd fly over the mountain roads. The others would say, 'She's crazy.' At places like the Pikes Peak hill climb, she'd make up all her time in the most difficult part of the mountains. She'd do things no man would ever do." At one point, Evelyn bought the famous James Bond Aston Martin, the DB5, and she "drove like crazy through mountains along sides of the embankment," adds Nonny, who felt Evelyn "was really at one with a car."

Having established a connection with the Sante Fe area of New Mexico in the late 1940s, the Mulls eventually moved there full time, settling on a rambling ranch outside of Espanola. Their daughters made the move as well, married, and gave them a great many grandchildren. As Evelyn had learned to drive at eleven, she made a point of teaching them at roughly the same age, instructing them on the finer points of double-clutching, doing a 360 and accelerating through curves in her 1956 Jaguar XK150. On holidays she was ringmaster of the wild menagerie at the ranch, presiding over rides and races on go-carts, motorcycles, horses, and snowmobiles—but only the fastest ones. "She didn't like you to be afraid," her granddaughter Cary says. "She always said, 'If I'd been born later, I would have been an astronaut.'" Initially wanting to stock the ranch with giraffes, she was only dissuaded when the local vet said he would refuse to treat the African animals. She settled for llamas instead.

John died at seventy-one in 1972. Thereafter, Evelyn's eccentricities, as well as her fondness for tippling, increased, fueling ever more outrageous behavior. She got a particular kick out of drag racing young Latinos on the streets of Espanola. All her grandchildren remember hiding in mortification in the back of Evelyn's special Mercedes, a rare sedan with a turbo-charged limo engine, as she'd pull up to a stoplight, eye a teenager in a low-rider through her brown driving glasses, and give him the thumbs-up for a drag race. She was well known by the local police, as she was frequently pulled over for speeding. But she generally got away with it. "They found her so interesting," granddaughter Cary remembers. "They'd sit there talking about cars for twenty minutes. She'd always say, 'It's so hard to go slow,' and they'd let her go." Evelyn died at seventy-six in 1989.

Her racing star having fallen as quickly as it had shot her to the heights of the women's game, Ruth Levy truly did not know what to do. "I was lost," she admits about a period when she went to a Beverly Hills shrink every morning for seven years and was prone to inhabit altered states more than occasionally. She sang in little boîtes around town, and quite well, too, according to those who heard her. In 1971, she decided to quit Los Angeles altogether. "I wanted out. I loaded up my Jeep and dog and came to Pagosa Springs," a real cowboy town in southern Colorado where her daughter Pam went to high school. Ruth had an art studio in town and a cabin up in

the mountains where she lived the full-bore countercul-
ture life, doing acid, sneaking down to town to jump
nude into the sulphur springs spa at four in the morning,
and hanging out with a rowdy bunch that included both
hard-drinking local cowboys and hardcore bikers from
nearby Bayfield; she found out from them that "I didn't
belong on two wheels." She was married to a local man,
Martin Martinez, for the decade she was there, but she
sums up this period of her life as "Hippies run loose." She
eventually married a third time, to Wayne "Hog" Raymond from Lubbock, Texas—he was nicknamed for his
motorcycle obsession but that changed to racing bikes—
and they have lived for years in the Danish-style tourist
town of Solvang, California, where she continues to paint,
pen poetry, and remain vitally engaged with everything
she finds interesting in the world.

Ruth always says that, of the 1950s group of women
racing drivers, "Denise could have been the only one to
go all the way." From the point of view of talent, intelligence, and guts, this rings true; if any American
woman of that time could have cut it as an international
race car driver of the first rank, it was Denise McCluggage. Denise went to, raced at, and reported from virtually every place in the world where cars are pitted
against one another, but the problem from her career
perspective was, "There wasn't anywhere else to go. I

was doing something from time to time because it was fun. I never raced what you called a full season. I never planned ahead, particularly. I'm a freelance, but I'm more free than lance. If I had been more organized in doing it, if there had been an actual career plan, then perhaps I could have pursued it more diligently, but there wasn't. It was something I did because it was there and I liked it.

"Indy didn't become a possibility until ten years later," Denise points out. "And that was only because someone wanted a chance and went looking for it. If I had still been driving, it would have been me. But Janet Guthrie was ten years younger, and she was more serious about it than I was."

Stressing that the changes on the American racing scene came on slowly and gradually, only to then be felt in their enormity almost overnight, Denise insists that, "The key changes were signaled by sponsorship. At first it made sense, they were more or less in-kind tradeoffs involving oil, tire, and car companies, then macho brands of beer and cigarettes. Gradually—and NASCAR was in the forefront of this—officials started realizing that car racers were attracting family audiences, or at least couples, so you started seeing ads for laundry detergents and soaps and things aimed at women and housewives, then the jackets and hats.

"I knew things were changing when I drove my Ferrari from New York City to Chicago, all alone, no mechanic, for a race at Meadowdale and I saw that my competition, two Corvettes, had arrived on a double-decked trailer. I said, 'Oh no, this is different.' I knew I'd never be able to compete with that. Plus, I drove there, raced, and drove home on one set of tires. You could drive a whole season on one set of tires. Now it costs as much to do one race as it did then for a whole season."

Denise's professional circumstances changed drastically as well between 1958 and 1959. In February 1958, two months after her Nassau triumph, Denise returned to the Caribbean to cover, but not drive in, the second Cuban Grand Prix, where her being on the scene in Havana gave her the biggest scoop of her journalism career. The country was in tumult, with the dictator Batista's regime feeling the heat from Fidel Castro's rebels on a steadily increasing basis. Many thought the race would be canceled or sabotaged, and the drivers arriving from around the world, including many of the sport's biggest names, were offered bodyguards. Tensions ran so high that the Swedish driver Joakim Bonnier—another of Ruth Levy's sometime beaux—was arrested simply because his beard made him resemble Castro.

There was a bad omen when a Cuban driver was killed in practice; the year before, many spectators had been badly hurt when a rickety course overpass had collapsed. On February 23, the night before the race, several drivers were mingling with a gaggle of fans and onlookers in the lobby of the Lincoln Hotel when Juan Manuel Fangio, the five-time world champion and the most famous sports figure in the Spanish-speaking world, had a gun stuck in his ribs by a bearded young man. A second gunman disarmed a nearby bodyguard and held the crowd at bay while an obedient Fangio was taken to a waiting car, in which he was spirited away.

By being on the scene, Denise was able to break the story of this audacious gambit in the United States in the *Herald Tribune*. All sides pointed fingers at the others as being the culprits behind Fangio's kidnapping, which worked just as Castro's revolutionaries had hoped, by bringing attention to their cause just as it enormously embarrassed the government during a big international event. As a manhunt continued fruitlessly, the race was delayed by two hours in the hopes that Fangio might appear, but when he didn't it got underway before a crowd of more than 150,000, while Fangio watched on television in the company of his kidnappers. It didn't last long, however. A novice Cuban driver, Armando Garcia Cifuentes, who by rights should not have been racing, lost control of his Testa Rossa on the sixth lap, causing it to jump a curb and crash into the stands, killing at least eight people and injuring about thirty-five; the government never provided definitive figures. The race was then stopped, with Stirling Moss declared the winner because he was ahead at the time. As for Fangio, he was quietly released to the Argentine ambassador and ironically became a bigger celebrity than ever in the United States, receiving the keys to the city of Miami and appearing on *The Ed Sullivan Show* thanks to his having endured the kidnapping by rebels.

Fangio only drove in two more major races, Monza at the end of June and Rheims at the beginning of July, before retiring, and Denise was there for both of them. But her perfect life at the *Herald Tribune* was coming to an end, as a new sports editor made it clear his first order of business was getting rid of this dame sports writer. It was complicated; he tried to send her to the women's page, Denise naturally refused, the union stepped in, and on and on. But there clearly could be no happy ending to the situation, so in midsummer Denise got involved on the ground floor of a new publication, *Competition Press*, edited by Don Stewart, which would allow—nay, encourage—her to drive in and report on races wherever she wanted. What she wanted, in fact, was to drive at Le Mans that year. Three-time Le Mans winner and long-time Ferrari rep Luigi Chinetti proposed his friend for his team and submitted the required documents. The reply from French officials was terse and unconditional: "This is an invitational race and we do not choose to invite women." It was enough to knock the wind out of anyone, as well as a strong hint that it would not be easy for Denise to join the ranks of her male driver friends on either the European or the American circuits.

She went to Le Mans anyway to cover it for *Competition Press* and was thus with Phil Hill for his and Olivier Gendebien's great victory in the wettest race in the history of the event, when it rained for twenty of the twenty-four hours. She continued on to Monza and Rheims, where Luigi Musso was killed, but was back in the States to take a win driving at Cumberland. In December she returned once again to Nassau, to find the party scene more frenetic than ever, to the point that it eclipsed the racing. "It wasn't too hot. Not like last year," she complained. Partly, it could have been sour grapes, as her car, Jim Lowe's Lotus, let her down. In the first ladies' heat, against eight competitors, she was in second place behind Evelyn Mull's Lotus when her gear remained in neutral when she shifted, which put her off the road and unable to restart. Evelyn's engine soon started to sputter, allowing Marion Lowe, also in a Lotus, to move ahead and win by forty-five seconds over Evelyn, with Pinkie Windridge third in an Alfa Veloce.

Having repaired the shift lever, Denise took the lead in

the second heat for good by the third lap, but as she couldn't win the overall due to her non-finish in the first heat, it came down to a battle between Evelyn and Marion, with Evelyn needing to make up her forty-five-second deficit from the first running to win. Evelyn poured it on but Marion stayed where she needed to be and finished forty-three seconds behind Evelyn in third for the overall win.

Denise noted that Nassau organizer Red Crise was writing his event's obituary by refusing to pay top drivers their asking price—1957 winner Stirling Moss was in attendance but not racing because Crise wouldn't pay him his $2000 fee—and insisting that he didn't need "name" drivers. But while Lance Reventlow and Pedro Rodriguez came into their own at Nassau in 1958 and some of the regulars continued to show up for the good times, Nassau began a genuine decline the following December when Sebring snared all the attention by staging the first United States Grand Prix since 1916.

Denise kept on going and going, and is still going. Her most unlikely pairing, perhaps, was with tenor sax player Allen Eager. A good-looking, restless hipster whose ever-shifting interests, along with drugs, might have prevented him from fulfilling his potential in any one field, he launched his musical career as a teenager during the war years and at eighteen was a fixture in New York's

52nd Street clubs. A proponent of bebop deeply influenced by Lester Young, he recorded with Gerry Mulligan and Terry Gibbs, played with Charlie Parker, lived in Paris for a while, and joined Timothy Leary at Harvard for early LSD trips. Meeting Denise while engaged to another woman, he shared her interest in skiing (for her part, Denise wrote a Zen-oriented book on the subject called *The Centered Skier*) as well as in cars. She says that when she met him in January 1961, "Allen wanted to do two things—to be in a Western and to drive a race car." Denise was able to help him in one of the two pursuits. She judged him a good driver to start with but made him more than that; at the end of the year, Denise and Allen entered her Ferrari 250 in the 12 Hours of Sebring and they won, not only their class, but also the Grand Turismo category. They took tenth overall, and $2000 in the bargain. It was Allen's first race. Subsequently, they raced Germany's imposing Nurburgring together, and the next year Sebring again, where they ran into Denise's old buddy Steve McQueen, on the verge of international stardom. Her alliance with Allen also brought her closer to her beloved jazz scene, and for a while she became Miles Davis's unofficial sports car advisor on his frequent purchases of expensive exotics.

Denise never married again or had kids. But her life has continued as an amazing patched-together adventure with cars always at the center of it. In January 2007, she turned eighty, and she still writes and drives, drives and writes. Looking back on the extraordinary decade of her youthful entrance into sports car driving, Denise, whose rigorous intelligence resists nostalgia just as it acknowledges it, allows that "We always thought, if we only had more money, we could have better cars and better races. But then we found that if there's too much money, it changes the nature of things. Still, either things change or they die. And if things never change, there's no nostalgia.

"In every endeavor, we have a tendency to advance things to the professional level. Even amateurs. The very first flush of the first time of doing something goes away very quickly. We do kill things out of love. We can improve things, we can do this, we can do that. The fun often gets changed into 'What can we do?' and we invent more rules and regulations. You have to enjoy it while it's there."

SELECT BIBLIOGRAPHY

BOOKS

Beaulieu, Lord Montagu of. *The Gordon Bennett Races.* London: Cassell, 1963.

Beaumont, Charles and William F. Nolan, eds. *An Omnibus of Speed: An Introduction to the World of Motor Sport.* New York: G.P. Putnam's Sons, 1958.

Benson, Michael. *Women in Racing.* Philadelphia: Chelsea House Publishers, 1997.

Bochroch, Albert R. *American Automobile Racing: An Illustrated History.* New York: A Studio Book, The Viking Press, 1974.

Bullock, John. *Fast Women: The Drivers Who Changed the Face of Motor Racing.* London: Robson Books, 2002.

Burnside, Tom; text by Denise McCluggage. *American Racing: Road Racing in the 50s and 60s.* Cologne: Konemann, 1996.

Davis, S.C.H. *Atalanta: Women As Racing Drivers.* London: G.T. Foulis & Co., Ltd., 1955.

Donaldson, Gerald. *Fangio: The Life Behind the Legend.* London: Virgin Books, 2003.

Evans, Art. *The Fabulous Fifties: Sports Car Races in Southern California.* Redondo Beach, CA: Photo Data Research, 2002.

―――. *Paramount Ranch Remembered.* Redondo Beach, CA: Photo Data Research, 2006.

―――. *Race Legends of the Fabulous Fifties.* Redondo Beach, CA: Photo Data Research, 2003.

Frankau, Gilbert. *Christopher Strong.* New York: E.P. Dutton, 1932.

Friedman, Dave. *The Legends of Motorsport.* M.R.I. Publications, 1992.

Hemingway, Ernest. *Death in the Afternoon.* New York: Charles Scribner's Sons, 1932.

Jarrott, Charles. *Ten Years of Motors and Motor Racing.* London: E. Grant Richards, 1906; subsequently reprinted 1912, 1927, 1956.

Lewis, Peter. *Motor Racing Through the Fifties.* London: Naval & Military Press, 1992.

Ludvigsen, Karl. *Juan Manuel Fangio: Motor Racing's Grand Master.* Newbury Park, CA; Sparkford, Nr Yeovil, Somerset: Haynes Publishing, 1999.

Lynch, Michael T., William Edgar and Ron Parravano. *American Sports Car Racing in The 1950s.* Osceola, WA: MBI Publishing Company, 1998.

McCluggage, Denise. *By Brooks Too Broad for Leaping.* Santa Fe: Fulcorte Press, 1994.

Miller, Peter. *The Fast Ones.* London: Stanley Paul, 1962.

Moss, Stirling, face to face with Ken Purdy. *All but My Life.* New York: E.P. Dutton & Co.,1963.

Mull, Evelyn. *Women in Sports Car Competition.* New York: Sports Car Press, 1958.

Naud, Elinor, ed. *Ladies, Start Your Engines: Women Writers on Cars and the Road.* Boston: Faber and Faber, 1996.

Nisley, Richard, ed. *If Hemingway Had Written A Racing Novel: The Best of Motor Racing Fiction: 1950-2000.* Reno: VelocePress, 2004.

Nolan, William F. *Carnival of Speed: True Adventures in Motor Racing.* New York: G.P. Putnam's Sons, 1973.

———. *Phil Hill: Yankee Champion: First American to Win the Driving Championship of the World.* Original edition, New York: G.P. Putnam's Sons, 1962; second, revised edition, Carpinteria, CA: Brown Fox Press, 1996.

O'Neil, Terry. *The Bahamas Speed Weeks.* Dorchester, England: Veloce Publishing Ltd., 2006.

Pollack, Bill. *Red Wheels and White Sidewalls: Confessions of An Allard Racer.* Carpinteria, CA: Brown Fox Books, 2004.

Radosta, John S. *The New York Times Complete Guide to Auto Racing.* Chicago: Quadrangle Books, 1971.

Ramsey, Alice Huyler. *Alice's Drive; Republishing Veil, Duster, and Tire Iron.* Tucson: The Patrice Press, 2004; annotated by Gregory M. Franzwa.

———. *Veil, Duster, and Tire Iron.* Pasadena: Castle Press, 1961.

Rasmussen, Henry. *European Sports Cars of the Fifties.* Arroyo Grande, CA: Arroyo Grande Press, 1978.

Scharff, Virginia Joy. *Taking the Wheel: Women and the Coming of the Motor Age.* New York: The Free Press, 1991.

Seymour, Miranda. *The Bugatti Queen: In Search of A Motor-Racing Legend.* London, New York: Simon & Schuster, 2004.

Stone, William S. *A Guide to American Sports Car Racing.* Garden City, NY: Doubleday & Company, 1960, 1963, 1967.

White, Gordon Eliot. *Lost Race Tracks: Treasures of Automobile Racing.* Hudson, WI: Iconografix, 2002.

Williams, Richard. *Enzo Ferrari: A Life.* London: Yellow Jersey Press, 2002.

ARTICLES

"A.A.A. Puts Ban on Road Runs," *Los Angeles Times,* May 21, 1916.

"All Enthusiastic," *Los Angeles Times,* January 9, 1910. Article about women racing at Ascot in Los Angeles.

Barry, David. "The Lady and the Talbot," *Sports Car International*, June/July 1999. Article about Linda Scott.

Blunk, Frank M. "Motor Car Sports," *The New York Times*, January 9, 1957. Profile of Evelyn Mull.

———. "Motor Car Sports," *The New York Times*, January 15, 1958. Walter Hansgen, Evelyn Mull named best drivers of 1957.

"'Bud' Currie, Mechanician, is Second Victim," *Stockton Record*, March 6, 1918.

"'Consider the Element of Safety,' Says Leslie Murray to Motorists," *Stockton Record*, March 5, 1918.

Covello, Mike. "The Golden Days of Thompson Raceway," *Vintage Motorsport*, March/April 1999.

Cuneo, Mrs. Andrew. "Why There Are So Few Women Automobilists," *Country Life in America*, 1908.

Edgar, William. "Mama Ruth: Fast Porsche Pilot of the 1950s," *Excellence*, September 2005. Article about Ruth Levy.

———. "The Roaring Springs—Part I," *Vintage Motorsport*, November/December 2003. Article about Palm Springs racing, 1950-1955.

———. "Oh, The Roaring Springs!—Part II," *Vintage Motorsport*, January/February 2004. Article about Palm Springs racing, 1956-1958.

Finlay, David. "Women in Motorsport," *CarKeys*, September 26, 2002.

"First Women's Auto Race in History," *Los Angeles Times*, February 4, 1918.

Fitch, John. "Remembering Briggs Cunningham," *Vintage Motorsport*, September/October 2003.

Goodwin, Carl. "The Aesthetics of Sport," *Vintage Motorsport*, November/December 2001. Article about Jim Kimberly.

———. "One Great Ride," *Vintage Motorsport*, May/June 2000. Article about Bridgehampton.

———. "Think Pink," *Vintage Motorsport*," March/April 2005. Profile of Donna Mae Mims.

"Hands Off! Curves Belong to Girls Too," *The Nassau Daily Tribune*, December 7, 1957. About Levy, McCluggage, Mull at Bahamas Speed Week.

Harris, Sonja. "Roaring into the Twenties: The Story of the Speederettes, Female Automobile Racers of the 1910s and 1920s." Fall 2003, unpublished.

Heimann, John B. "The Life and Death of Riverside International Raceway—Part I," *Vintage Motorsport*, January/February 2002.

———. "The Life and Death of Riverside International Raceway—Part II," *Vintage Motorsport*, March/April 2002.

———. "Roar by the Ocean," *Vintage Motorsport*, November/December 2002. Article about 1950's racing in Santa Barbara.

"The History of Women in the Automotive World," *Road & Travel*, April 3, 2006.

"Housewife, 25, Portraitist and Racer of Sports Autos," *Los Angeles Times*, October 21, 1956. Article about Ruth Levy.

"Hubby's Hobby Hepped Horsewoman to Car Racing; Only Lady Entry at Walterboro," *The Charleston Evening Post*, March 12, 1956. Profile of Evelyn Mull.

"In Auto Racing You Need Nerves of Ice," *Los Angeles Times*, June 21, 1959. Article about Josie von Neumann.

"Italians Pay a Tribute to Dead Driver," *Stockton Record*, March 5, 1918.

"The Ladies Stole the Show on Saturday," *The Nassau Guardian*, December 9, 1957. Report on Levy-McCluggage showdown at Nassau.

Levine, Robert. "King of the Road," *Vanity Fair*, July, 2006. Profile of Carroll Shelby.

Lynch, Michael T. "A Car Enthusiast Comes to America," *Vintage Motorsport*, March/April 2003. Article about John von Neumann.

———. "A Fast Free Spirit," *Vintage Motorsport*, September/October 2005. Article about Bob Drake.

"Man Must Start San Diego Race," *Los Angeles Times*, March 23, 1916. Article about A.A.A. barring women from any participation in upcoming race at San Diego Exposition.

"Miss Vitagliano, 'Speederette,' Says Women Can Drive in Races as Well as Men-Chats on Aims," *Stockton Record*, March 2, 1918.

"Mrs. Wolfelt Wins Stinson Trophy Race; Little Woman in White is Ascot Star," *Los Angeles Times*, February 4, 1918.

Newton, Harry. "A Silver Spoon and a Lead Foot," *Vintage Motorsport*, September/October 2000. Article about Bruce Kessler.

New York Herald Tribune, 1956-1959. Regular by-lined articles and columns by Denise McCluggage.

"Nina Vitagliano is Killed in Auto Races on Local Track," *Stockton Record*, March 4, 1918.

Obert, Genevieve. "Fast Women of the '50s," *Vintage Motorsport*, November/December 2002.

"Ruth Wightman Tells How to Become a Speederette," *Los Angeles Times*, February 3, 1918.

"Speederettes are Ready for Starting Gun," *Stockton Record*, March 2, 1918.

"Sporting Chance is Women Racers' Plea," *Los Angeles Times*, January 29, 1918.

"Sports Car Champ Says Her Husband Is Grand," *The Sunday Sun* (New Jersey), January 26, 1958. Article about Evelyn Mull.

"Tomboy with a Typewriter," *Time*, April 3, 1957. Column about Denise McCluggage.

"To Ship Dead Woman's Body," *Stockton Record*, March 4, 1918.

Towle, Herbert Ladd. "The Woman at the Wheel," *Scribner's Magazine*, February, 1915.

"Woman Driver Proves Colors with Plymouth," *Los Angeles Times*, April 28, 1957. Article about Mary Davis and the Mobil Gas Economy Run.

"Woman Racing Driver Killed," *Los Angeles Times*, March 4, 1918. Article about death of Nina Vitagliano Torre in Stockton race.

"Woman Set to Drive in Grand Prix Race," *Los Angeles Times*, October 6, 1959. Article about Josie von Neumann.

"Women Barred from This Year's Glidden Tour," *Los Angeles Times*, July 11, 1909.

"Yesterday's Fatal Accident at the Stockton Race Track Was Avoidable," *Stockton Record*, March 4, 1918.

FILMS/TV SHOWS

Fast Women, 45-minute documentary produced by Rachel Belofsky and directed by Laurie Agard, 2000.

Films of the Fabulous Fifties, four-disk compilation by Al Moss of mostly color, home-movie racing footage of the 1950's and early 1960's shot at Carrell Speedway, Grand Central (Glendale), Hansen Dam, Laguna Seca,

March Field, Palm Springs, Paramount Ranch, Pebble
Beach, Pomona, Riverside, Santa Ana, Santa Barbara,
and Torrey Pines. *RacerMoss@esedona.net.*

Girl Racers, four-part documentary series from Global TV
(Canada), Part One first broadcast in Canada July 8,
2005, in the United States on Biography Channel September 15, 2005.

WEBSITES

141.com/vir2004. Account of the Women in Racing tribute,
June 10–13, 2004, at Virginia International Raceway,
Alton, Virginia.

ausbcomp.com. "What Was the First Car? Quick History
of the Automobile for Young People," by William W.
Bottorff.

autosport.com. Auto Sports Magazine.

awmn.com.au. The Australian Women's Motorsport Network.

brdc.co.uk. British Racing Drivers' Club.

briggscunningham.com.

brooklands-automobilia-regalia-collectors-club.co.uk

brooklandstrack.co.uk. The Brooklands Society.

btinternet.com. Women in motorsports timeline from
1899.

bwrdc.co.uk. British Women's Racing Drivers' Club.

clevelandparklife.intheteam.com. History of Middlebrough Speedway, 1928-1996.

d.david.com/formula 1/race. "The Story of the Grand Prix," including Charles Jarrott's account of the 1903 Paris-Madrid race.

diamonds.mcc.org.uk. Profiles of women motorcycle riders.

dwdracing.com. Account of the Women in Racing tribute at Virginia International Speedway.

formula1.com.

grandprix.com.

greatdreams.com. Women's accomplishments in diverse fields.

historicracing.com.

justmidgets.homestead.com. Photo article on Fay Taylour.

lemans.org.

mi5.gov.uk. Intelligence on Fay Taylour.

motorcycle-uk.com. Vintage Motorcycle Magazine.

motorsport.com.

motorsporthalloffame.com.

motorsportmemorial.org.

motorstv.com. Motors TV Network.

nascar.com.

northnet.org.stlawrenceaauuv/timeline.htm. Women sports landmarks timeline.

racingarchives.org. International Motor Racing Research Center at Watkins Glen.

radio.cz.en/article/58031. "Eliska Junkova: the Czech Racing Queen of the Jazz Age."

roadrunning.com. "An Automotive E-zine," edited by Denise McCluggage.

september8th.com. Dedicated to "reliving motorsports' past."

speedqueens.mysite.wandaloo-members.co.uk.

statesecrets.co.uk. Information on Fay Taylour's political affiliations.

theautochannel.com.

VeloceToday.com. "The Online Magazine for Italian Car Enthusiasts."

vintagespeedway.homestead.com.

wsrp.wz.cz/natus.html. Statistics on U.S. national races (from 1948).

ACKNOWLEDGMENTS

I was introduced to the world of women racers during a Thanksgiving dinner at the New Mexico ranch of Ellie and Peter Bickley, parents of their daughter and my friend, Cary Bickley Zeltser. A photo on the wall—as it happens, the racing photo ultimately used for the cover of this book—piqued my curiosity. After I'd heard a few stories about the elegant driver in the picture, Cary's late grandmother, Evelyn Mull, and seen the family's rare copy of her little book, *Women in Sports Car Competition*, I knew I'd come across a subject worthy of some significant further research.

Serendipitously, it turned out that Denise McCluggage, the most proficient woman driver of her era, lived nearby in Santa Fe. When I called her out of the blue, she graciously invited me over, launching a series of encounters—lunches, dinners, interviews, phone conversations, weekly gatherings of her Car Table gearheads, and, most memorably, test driving a hot new Audi with her in the hills outside Santa Fe—that I hope continues indefinitely. Her feisty, clear-headed, entirely original intelligence was immediately striking and continues to be so. Her intellectual curiosity is such that, along with her prolific ongoing writing career and the constant offers she receives (and accepts) to participate in automotive events around the world, she would need two or three lifetimes to accomplish all she wants to do. Her writing is still far too-little known outside racing circles, and I hope she can soon clear the time to properly write her own story, one of the great contemporary lives I've encountered.

I thank Denise for her exceptional generosity in answering so many questions about the past, when she has the present so forcefully on her mind. I also thank the Bickleys for their unceasing hospitality, in Espanola and elsewhere, as well as for their time in granting interviews and tracking down information on Evelyn Mull's racing career. Along with Cary, Ellie and Peter, family members who helpfully and amusingly provided memories of their lively ancestor included Louisiana Longwell, Marion Mills, Frank Black, and Cary Black Spier.

Among the other women drivers, Ruth Levy Raymond, Mary Davis, and Ginny Sims, all spry, vigorous, and looking far younger than their years, repeatedly had me to their homes in Southern California, plied me with stories about their great racing days and entrusted me with photographs and memorabilia. Non-driving Cal Club fixture Mary O'Connor was also most helpful, while racers Linda Scott and Suzy Dietrich provided useful information.

Among the men, Bill Pollack has been an unending source of witty and wise guidance to the events of fifty years ago. As genial a man as he is a sparkling writer—his *Red Wheels and White Sidewalls: Confessions of an Allard Racer* rates as the liveliest personal memoir of the Fabulous Fifties yet composed—Bill generously shared information, invited me to Cal Club gatherings, and made invaluable comments on the manuscript.

This project caused me to cross paths once again with Bruce Kessler, who had crucially helped on the *Red Line 7000* section of my biography of Howard Hawks. Other '50s figures who provided interviews and/or useful information and photographs included Tom Burnside, Tim Considine, Chuck Daigh, Will Edgar, Bill Gardner, Carl Goodwin, Robert E. Griffin, Jack McAfee, Donna Mae Mims, and Bob Tronolone. Stirling Moss spoke with me in London, and I subsequently had the extraordinary surprise of encountering him again completely by chance in the pits at Laguna Seca. And then there is the incomparable Jim Sitz, who began attending '50s racing events as a youngster out of sheer enthusiasm and seems to remember the precise vehicles and finishing order of every race he's seen over the subsequent fifty-five years; the term encyclopedic memory should be reserved exclusively for him.

I want to thank self-confessed petrolhead Jeremy Thomas for introducing me to John Bernard, who provided a dream come true by hosting me at his flat right above the course for the Monaco Classics races in May 2006, which provided a flashback to my youthful first exposure to Grand Prix racing, at Brands Hatch, in 1970.

Sincere appreciation also to Julie Allen, Monica Corcoran, Bill Green, and Bill King of the International Motor Racing Center at Watkins Glen, Randy Riggs, Mike Silverman for arrangements in Carmel and continued good cheer, and Lisa Weinstein.

Dorna Khazeni performed outstanding feats of research and legwork at crucial moments to make everything possible, and Charles Higham was, as always, an unerring source of insight and expert advice on all matters literary.

This book would not have been remotely possible without the unwavering support and latitude of my editor at *Variety*, Peter Bart, who provides an extraordinary model of discipline and achievement for anyone fantasizing about doing two or three jobs at once.

At Miramax Books, I am grateful to the former editor-in-chief, Jonathan Burnham, for his initial attraction to *Fast Women*. Since then, Rob Weisbach, JillEllyn Riley,

Judy Hottensen, and Kristin Powers have offered stead-fast belief in the book and laudable patience for an author not as fast as his subjects.

I cannot sufficiently thank my agent, Dan Strone, who was always there when it counted and whose intuition, analyses and guidance have invariably proven correct.

Most of all, I thank my wife, Sasha Alpert, and daughter Madeleine, for so agreeably tolerating the presence of so many other exciting women in my life for so long, and my son Nicholas.